*Loving me isn't selfish;
it's the foundation of all meaningful connections*

LOVING ME MEANS MORE THAN ANYTHING

LATORIA DANIELLE

DISCLAIMER

This is a work of creative non-fiction. All of the events in this memoir are true to the best of the author's memory. Some names and identifying features have been changed to protect the identity of certain parties. The views expressed in this memoir are solely those of the author.

©Copyright 2024 Latoria Danielle.
All Rights Reserved.

Photography by Jayor Photography

DEDICATION

To my children who suffered the most through this, I love you. Together, we will heal through transparency, forgiveness, and love. Mommy loves you forever and always!

LOVING ME MEANS MORE THAN ANYTHING

TABLE OF CONTENTS

1. The Back Story 1
2. Daddy's Little Girl 3
3. How It All Started 6
4. He Was the Perfect Stranger 15
5. This Isn't Life 18
6. War Room 26
7. My Vision 30
8. Finding Me 39
9. The Final Straw 45
10. No Angel 58
11. After the Separation 66
12. I Can't Believe This 76
13. My Chapter Continues 87

CHAPTER ONE

THE BACK STORY

IN 2017, I WENT THROUGH ONE OF THE MOST TRAUMATIC experiences of my life. The pain that I experienced was one that I had never experienced before, and I didn't know how I was going to make it out alive. I was filled with so many emotions that life became overwhelming. I couldn't handle it mentally or physically, and spiritually, I was dead. For the first time in my life, I was lost for words. Every time I tried to express myself, I fell deeper and deeper into a state of depression and anger, so deep that I didn't even recognize myself.

It felt like being at the beach on a beautiful, sunny day, with a clear sky and warm water. The water feels so good that you keep inching yourself further and further away from the shore. Then, out of nowhere, a wave hits you. Instantly, you find yourself fighting for your life. The water keeps rising higher and higher up your neck, and suddenly, you are being consumed by a force that you can't control. You try to fight, but no matter how hard you try to stay above the water, it consumes you. All I wanted was peace, but peace no longer entertained me, and the beast within me was roaring. I found myself backed into a corner fighting to survive. I was lost and needed to be found. I needed help.

There were so many times that I wanted to lash out on social media. You know, tell my side of the story. Get my point across, but God silenced me. My words were garbled. My face was drenched with tears each time I attempted to explain why I needed to be saved, not my marriage. I didn't need another prayer or scripture. But here is the light: "I was being shaken, broken, and remolded by the Potter's Hands. He had placed a hedge of protection over me. A secret place where God would catch all of my tears. A tabernacle of peace."

I was safe, but I didn't even know it because the things that I wrestled with tugged at my spirit until they consumed me. I was prepared to walk in my divine purpose. Everything that I had learned had to be stripped away from me so that God could use me how He wanted to use me.

Every time I felt the water going above my head, I grabbed my laptop and typed. Keystroke after keystroke, my strength was restored, and my anger subsided. The more I typed, the more God loosened my bounds.

Often, we are afraid to speak out about what we're going through. The fear of judgment clouds us and restricts us from verbalizing the pain that we have endured. It's never easy being vulnerable or transparent, but I found my healing in telling my story. I hope that you get something out of this as well. If not, I pray you continue to seek the help that you need. And maybe, one day, you will come back and say, "Ah, that's what Latoria Danielle meant." I encourage you to walk in what is true to you. Do not deviate from that path. It is liberating, and it is yours to walk.

CHAPTER TWO

DADDY'S LITTLE GIRL

THE HARDEST PART IN THIS JOURNEY IS STARTING, RECALLING memories that you'd rather just forget and start fresh. I know now that these memories are part of my foundation. I have no regrets, just moments that I'm glad are over. Some of which I hid, thinking that if I didn't address them, they'd disappear. That's not true.

I grew up with a "silver-handled spoon in my mouth," as my mother would say. I can honestly say that I never went without. My mother had three children, and I was my father's ninth child. Although I had so many siblings, it was like being the only child because when I was born, all my siblings were all grown except one. My parents made it a priority to make sure that I had everything that I needed and more. I lived with both of my parents until I was five. I never heard my father raise his voice at my mom, and they never argued in front of me. What seemed to be a great home apparently wasn't that great because my father moved out.

I can recall the night my father left as if it was yesterday. I remember his blue leather suitcase, white Ford F150, and my red onesie pajama set. The story didn't go as most would expect from an African-American man. You know the one where the father leaves the home and the mother and child never hear from him again? Or the one where the father plays "peek-a-boo" with the child. A game played with young children, which involves hiding behind something and suddenly reappearing, saying "peek-a-boo." I'm thankful to say that although the relationship didn't work out between my dad and my mom, my dad never missed a beat in my life.

My dad eventually ended up getting married and officially moved to Virginia. For years, my dad drove from Virginia to North Carolina after he got off work to keep me while my mom worked overnight. I was so excited when I heard his truck pull into the driveway. I can still remember the sound of his tires crushing the rocks in our driveway to this day. With excitement, I would run to the back door and wait patiently for him to turn the key in the knob. As soon as the door opened, I would immediately jump into his arms. He would greet me with the biggest hugs and kisses every time. Even now, as a thirty-two-year-old woman, I still greet him the same way. On days that my mom didn't cook, my dad cooked T-bone Steaks and eggs. It was all he knew how to cook at that time, and I loved it. When he didn't cook, he took me to McDonald's or Burger King where I ordered a plain cheeseburger and only ate the meat.

After my dad was done cooking, he would call me to the table. We would sit down and eat. He taught me how to use a steak knife, and together, we ate our steak. There were days when I wasn't all that hungry, but he made me sit at the table and watch him eat. I remember wanting to get up, but he insisted that I sit with him. And that's just what I did. My daddy and I did everything together. Some days, he came home exhausted and only wanted to take a nap. One can imagine what it is like after working eight hours out in the elements. He was tired, but I was a ball of energy. He would say, "Come on and lay down with Daddy. Daddy needs to rest his eyes." I knew he would eventually fall asleep because he was tired, and we'd lay down and take a nap together. He'd lay on his back and extend his arm out straight, and that's where I would lay until the snoring stopped. Sometimes, he'd make me move my head because he couldn't stand the smell of my hair grease. Back then, all my mom used was the thick blue Ultra Sheen in my hair. He hated it, and looking back now, Ultra Sheen is greasy and has a strong odor.

Everywhere my daddy went, I wanted to go. If he went to the bathroom, I would be right there sitting at the door waiting for him to come out. I didn't have anyone to play with, and all I had was my daddy. When my dad convinced my mom to let me go outside, we rode our bikes together. She didn't like me playing outside because she didn't want me to get dirty or scar my legs. My mom said that a woman is supposed to have pretty legs. Naturally, I fell off my bike a few times, but now, I can thank my mom for my gorgeous legs.

As I got older, my dad went from teaching me how to ride a bike to how to drive a car. He also taught me about the "Facts of Life," as he called it. Contrary to statistical analysis and his presence, that did not deter me from having two children before the age of eighteen and all of the other crazy stuff I experienced in between. I had one child at fourteen and the other at sixteen. While other outside factors contributed to how my life turned out, I had a great example of what a husband and father should be and what a family should look like. My parents were outstanding in my opinion, but I had my own story to write.

CHAPTER THREE
HOW IT ALL STARTED

IT'S STRANGE HOW WE MET. I WAS A TELLER AT A LOCAL BANK. He came to the bank on Fridays to deposit his checks. As often as he used to patronize the bank, I had never paid him any mind. I was working, and my focus was on processing the customers' transactions as quickly and accurately as possible. Friday afternoons at the bank were tiring and hectic. It seemed like everyone in the city was trying to cash their check. We had a line outside the door. I never entertained the idea of meeting anyone in the teller line.

There was enough going on in my personal life that adding another male to the equation wasn't a thought. I had just ended a causal relationship, and my focus was on my two babies and obtaining my bachelor's degree. Despite all the crazy things that had happened this particular year, I was doing well. I had recently purchased an all-black, two-door CLK 320 Mercedes Benz. My car had two seats in the front and two in the back, which was just enough for me and my two. I had a great career at the bank, and to top it off, I was offered an opportunity to take my children to Disney World. Taking my children to Disney World was something that I would have never imagined doing, especially since I had never gone before and the fact that I was a single parent. I felt like I was sitting on top of the world. A co-worker and her family were taking a family trip, and she invited me to come along. Thank you, Mr. and Mrs. Chandler.

New car. Tax money. School refund money. Steady paycheck. I was more financially stable than I had ever been in my life, and I made sure that my children reaped the benefits of it.

When this guy came in the bank, he made small talk here and there. One day, during his transaction, he slid me a little note that said, "I want to tell you something," with a smiley face drawn at the bottom. If you have ever worked at a bank, you know that there are different types of bank robbers, and one of them is called the *Note Passer Robber*—the robber who robs the bank with a note.

I chuckled inside my head. I thought it was funny. I knew he wasn't trying to rob the bank because he had an account with us and frequented the bank every Friday. I read it and threw it in the trash because I wasn't interested in anything about this man other than doing my job. Besides all my bad luck with men, he just wasn't my type. He came in with a dirty white t-shirt, baggy jeans that sagged off his hips, and flip-flops with socks. Now, I know what you are thinking, *Girl, you are crazy. That man was dirty because he was working! That meant he actually had a job.* Okay, maybe, but I still wasn't interested! For several weeks, he continued to write notes with the same message, including his phone number. And those, too, went in the trash. Having conversations with the customers made the bankers appear friendly and that we had great interest in our customers; I was just doing my job.

One day, our conversation took a positive turn. He mentioned that he wanted to open a group home for young boys, and then he had my full attention! I was a teenage parent twice. I came from a small town, so I understood the hardship of being a teenage parent and really wanted to help other girls not go down the same road as I did. From my hometown, it almost seemed like the norm, but not everyone had the same outcomes.

I realized that consistency, support, and resources were needed, so for a few years, I had been working on starting a non-profit organization for teenage mothers. As our conversation progressed, I realized that we had a lot in common. It was nice to talk to someone with a shared interest in giving back to the community, so this time, I saved the note and gave him my number for business purposes. I continued my day as usual and thought no more about him.

Some time had passed by, and I hadn't heard from the gentleman from the bank. Then suddenly, I received a random text message from him. I was on vacation with my family on our annual "Mother-Daughter Weekend"—a weekend where all my grandmothers' daughters and their daughters getaway. This year, we were in Williamsburg, Virginia. When I received the text, I was dealing with some personal issues. His text was inspirational and just what I needed to hear at that time, so I decided to respond.

Later that week, I called him and asked if he would like to go to the movies. I can't tell you why or even what I was thinking. Maybe I just needed some positive energy. Of course, he said yes. This was completely out of my norm. Me asking a man on a date? Yeah right! But it happened. I remember this night like it was yesterday. He had backed into my driveway with a beautiful black S-Class Mercedes Benz. He had told me that he had just brought a Mercedes, but by looking at him, I just assumed it was an old Mercedes and wasn't impressed again because he didn't look like somebody who could afford a Mercedes Benz. I knew that it was wrong of me to judge this man, but he was only making minimum wage. I cashed his checks, so I know.

When he pulled up in my driveway, he called to let me know that he was outside. I walked out of the house, and there he was, standing, waiting to open my car door. I thought to myself, this is a first. It made for a great first impression, especially since my father was standing in the window watching me get into the gentleman's car. My father later told this story at our first child's baby shower. He looked nothing like he looked at the bank. He cleaned up very well. I was now impressed.

That night, we saw the movie *Angels & Demons*. As I write this story almost ten years later, I honestly don't remember anything about the movie. Afterward, we went to eat. Everything was perfect. He drove me home afterward, and we sat in my driveway for a few minutes just talking. Neither of us wanted to part ways. We were having such a great time and even better conversation. It was getting late, and he had to go to work in the morning. For some reason, we opted to go back to his house that night. We slept in the same bed, but nothing happened sexually. However, it wasn't too much longer when it did. We began to see each other daily, and we grew even closer. Needless to say, the words, "group home" never came up again.

One day, later in our relationship, I decided that I wanted to keep his car and he kept mine. My CLS Mercedes Benz was a sports car, and his S430 Mercedes Benz was a lot larger, and I enjoyed the luxury of switching cars. I thought it was too cute. They were his-and-hers matching Benzes, and to make matters even better, they were both black! I love black cars. We both did. We discovered that we had both purchased our Benz around the same time before we even met. After I was done "playing" with his car that week, I called and told him that I wanted my car back. He said, "No." I was confused but didn't think much of it. Later that day, we met up to exchange cars. My car had a full tank of gas, and the airbag caution light was off! The man had put my car in the shop. I couldn't believe it! None of the men I had dated before fixed my car. My daddy was the only man that had ever done that. So, I was very impressed again. He was a man who took initiative.

He was very respectful and seemed to really be interested in dating me. It only seemed right that the people who meant the most to me met him. So, I eventually introduced him to my children. I never understood why some will date and not introduce their children to the person they are dating. I would rather know how my children are going to respond to a person before I fall in love with them. Our relationship can only thrive if he connects with my children. Being raised by a step-parent—I hate that term and we don't use them in our family—I had first-hand experience in understanding the importance of the bond between the two. I was a single parent, and my main priority was my children and providing a healthy, stable environment for them. It was hard-working full-time, raising kids, and trying to date. I didn't see any red flags, so I figured, why not?

Our first outing with the kids was at Mt. Trashmore in Virginia Beach, VA. There was a carnival at Mt. Trashmore while we were there, so everything just seemed perfect. The kids had a blast, and they appeared to really be getting along. He paid for everything and made sure that the kids enjoyed themselves.

The relationship between him and me escalated quickly, and within a month, I missed my period. I wasn't too sure how to feel about this because I already had two children and I didn't want any more. I was very open and honest with him about not wanting more children and shared with him that I had gotten an abortion before I met him. Before I got the abortion, I never thought that I would have one. I often ridiculed other women for doing the same thing that I had done. But at that time, I did what was in the best interest of me and my children. Now, I understand why it is so important not to judge other people based on their actions. You never know what someone may be going through and why they do the things that they do.

I trusted him because he knew what I had done and how important it was for me not to have any more children. I could have taken control and prevented this by not having unprotected sex, but I trusted him. We had both recently been tested for sexually transmitted diseases and shared our test results. I never thought he wouldn't use the withdrawal method to intentionally get me pregnant. I was young and dumb and now trapped in a relationship I didn't prepare for. I can recall his exact words while he was having an orgasm inside of me, "I want you to have my baby." It was at that moment that I knew that I was going to be pregnant. I was so sure that I waited a few weeks before going to my gynecologist to have a blood test done. Sure enough, I was pregnant. I couldn't put down on paper how I felt at that moment, but it didn't matter how I was feeling because there was nothing that I could do. I couldn't fathom going through another abortion. After all, abortion shouldn't be used as a form of contraceptive. Afterward, I rationalized that he was a hard worker and very dedicated to me. And we could make this work. He didn't have any children; he had never been married before, so why not give it a try? I had no choice but to give this my all because I decided to keep my baby. I had to face the reality that I was going to be a mother of three children. With that reality, I understood that no matter if my plan to make my new family work, I would be solely responsible for taking on this new life and decided that I would love my new child with all of me. My perception of having a new baby changed.

Later that day, I went to the Dollar Tree and grabbed some balloons, a gift bag, and a few baby items. I wanted to surprise him and tell him the great news. I just knew that he would be excited to find out that he was going to be a father for the first time. I rode around for a while, trying to come up with a creative way to tell him that he was going to be a father.

So, I went to Party City to purchase a bouquet of balloons, then I went to Dollar General and purchased a gender-neutral infant outfit and put it in a gift bag. I was incredibly excited to break the news to him.

After I completed all my shopping, I headed directly to his house. His apartment was very small. As soon as you open the front door, you are in the living room, and when you turn your head to the left, you'll see the kitchen. I could see that he wasn't in one of those two places, so I walked through the kitchen and into his bedroom. There, I found him sleeping. I walked over to the bed to wake him up and tell him about the news. He fussed about me waking him up. Dismissing the news about the baby, he rolled over and went back to sleep.

I couldn't believe that he responded that way. I was devastated and completely hurt. I was pregnant again and feeling like I was getting ready to be a single parent. I immediately walked out of the house in tears. I let the bouquet of balloons go and kept it moving. I couldn't go home upset, so I sat in my car in a parking lot down the street to try and get myself together.

Before I pulled off to go home, he called and asked me to come back to the house. He apologized, so I gave him what was left of the surprise, and our new chapter began. This was my fourth pregnancy but my first as an adult in a real relationship.

Unexpectedly, I became extremely sick, and one would think that I had never been pregnant before. Out of nowhere, my saliva became extremely thick, and I couldn't swallow it, so I had to carry around a bottle or cup to spit in everywhere I went. Even at night, when I couldn't possibly hold a bottle or cup to spit in, I still had to spit. I would have to place a folded towel under my head so the saliva could drain out of my mouth. This, mixed with severe nausea, became unmanageable, so I went to my doctor. He diagnosed me with ptyalism. I spit in a bottle every day during my pregnancy till two weeks after the pregnancy. It was horrible. I was prescribed a few medications to help, but nothing helped. I couldn't keep any food down, and I kept getting dehydrated, which led to multiple emergency room visits to get fluids in me.

The customers at the bank thought it was disgusting seeing me spit in a cup after every word during a transaction and were complaining to my branch manager. I couldn't blame them; I completely understood. On top of all of that, I was constantly being written up for not following the protocols that were set in place to secure the money at our teller stations because I kept leaving my drawers unlocked and cash exposed while I ran to the bathroom to vomit. I couldn't maintain their expectations as an employee, and I didn't want to be terminated, so I put in my two-week notice. Life just continued to go downhill from there. Eventually, I had to stop pursuing my dream of completing my bachelor's degree as well. The pregnancy took a huge toll on my body.

Without my job, I was stuck with depending on him to financially care for me. That was no problem for him. He took very good care of me financially. Emotionally would become the issue. He gave me a hundred dollars every week to buy whatever I needed. Although I never had to buy much, he still paid for all our food when we would go out to eat together, and he shopped for all my maternity clothes. He even bought foods he thought would make me feel better. With everything that was going on, getting married just seemed like it was the best decision for us to make. I wanted to give my children a full family. The two children that I had before meeting him had absent fathers. I felt as though they needed a man, outside of my dad, to be a father figure to them.

So, one day, we were out, and he asked me to take him to the bank. He insisted that we go to my old job. It was just around the corner from his house. We pulled up at the drive-through ATM. I asked him for his card to put in the ATM, and he told me no. I was offended. In my mind, I was saying, *"You trust me enough to get me pregnant but not enough to give me your debit card and PIN to make a withdrawal from the ATM? You've got to be kidding me!"* I just looked dumbfounded. Eventually, he got out of the car and walked to the ATM. I was still in disbelief when he turned around to me and asked me if I would marry him. We weren't at the ATM to withdraw money. We were there so that he could propose to me. He said that he wanted to ask me at the place where we first met. I said, "Yes." I was seven months pregnant and now newly engaged! This happened on a Friday. That following Monday, he woke up and said, "Let's go to the courthouse and get married." I had said yes to the engagement, so why not go ahead and get married. That is the whole purpose of the engagement, right? Well, we got up, got the kids dressed, and to the Norfolk courthouse, we went. In less than one month of meeting this man, I was pregnant, and in less than a year, I was married to the perfect stranger.

CHAPTER FOUR
HE WAS THE PERFECT STRANGER

LIFE STARTED PRETTY GOOD FOR TWO PEOPLE WHO REALLY didn't know each other. I guess we had the basics covered. He loved God, and so did I. He was a hard worker and loved his mother. At the time, we lived about five minutes from his mother's house. On Saturday mornings, he often cooked breakfast (the only thing he could cook), and he made her a plate and took it to her house. While he was there, he'd take out her trash as well as any other small odds and ends he could help her out with. I absolutely loved how he cared for her. He was sure to make a great husband, right? That's what they all say.

You've heard it before, "How he treats his mother is how he'll treat you." I don't know how true that is, but I soon learned that he might have been a great helper but he wasn't the most affectionate person in the world. This quilkly became a problem for me. I noticed that it was easy for him to ignore me and others around him, but I was in this thing too deep. One of the first conversations that I had with his mother was her telling me that her desire was for her children to all meet someone who loved them for them and that they would get married and be happy. I'll never forget that. I tried to do that and more.

After the wedding, the children and I officially moved in his house. We spent a lot of time there before the marriage but he didn't want us to move in until we got married. Once we moved in, things just kept unfolding, and layers of him just kept being exposed. I learned that he was still involved in illegal street activity. He was a felon, and I wanted no part of the street life. I only figured this out after our house got broken into right before Christmas. They stole all of my kids' Christmas gifts and all of the stuff that we had purchased for the arrival of our new baby. That further explained the minimum wage checks, the Mercedes Benz he owned, and how he so seamlessly financially provided for us on his wages. I had vowed to myself that I would never date a felon again. There were things I wanted to do like own a gun, adopt a baby one day, and maybe become a foster parent. None of this seemed to be in my future. Eventually, he left the streets alone, and the struggle got real. We cleared out our savings account and started our first business. One of my favorite things about him was that he was very clean. He would take multiple showers a day, and I loved it. But I soon discovered that he smoked cigarettes and was trying to hide it from me. The more I learned, the more I knew that I didn't really know him at all. This man was a manipulator, scammer, and liar.

The first year went by, and it was rough. I was used to raising my children on my own. It was hard for me to share my newborn baby with a stranger. We argued over the smallest things like how to hold the baby, how to bathe the baby, and how to use the aspirator to remove snot from the baby's nose. I almost had a heart attack watching him stick that long blue tube in my baby's nose. I told him that he needed to squeeze it first to remove all the air before he put it in her nose and not to stick it in too deep; that became a war. After arguing back and forth, he backed off and parented from afar right in the same home. I damaged him, and it set the precedent for the type of father he would be in the future. I regret that. My inability to trust him took away from his ability to have that hands-on experience with his first born. I was overbearing and a helicopter parent.

CHAPTER FIVE
THIS ISN'T LIFE

I CAN'T SAY THAT WE BECAME DISTANT, JUST DISTRACTED. A couple of months after our first child was born, he was laid off from his job. We decided that we would open a children's store. He mowed lawns on the side to keep money flowing. While out mowing one day, he came across a vacant retail location that seemed just right for us. The store was perfect in size, the rent was cheap, and I could swing it alone off minimal sales. We set up a bassinet and rocking chair beside our self-made register for our three-month-old, and I started working. I couldn't bear the thought of leaving my baby to go back to work, so this worked perfectly for me.

It took a few weeks for us to order inventory and set up, but everything seemed to be going very well for our small business. My husband had grown up with a candy lady in his neighborhood, so he also wanted to add snacks and drinks to our inventory. A while later, we expanded to women's clothing. The rent alone was so cheap that we could pay our rent with the money that we made off candy, snacks, and drinks from the neighborhood kids. The only issue we had with the building was the plumbing. The toilet kept backing up and overflowing. The landlord wasn't any help in getting this issue fixed, so we decided that we were going to move out of that location when our lease was up. So, when our lease was up at the store, my husband asked me if I wanted to get a larger retail space or a larger house. Sales were great, and our customer base was expanding. By this time, he was back working fulltime, and we had the resources to move one of the two ways but not both. The store was producing enough money to cover its own overhead.

At the time, we were living in a two-bedroom duplex with three children; we needed the space. We wrestled with the idea of moving in with his mom and getting a bigger store. We were doing well financially with the store, so I thought that we could expand our business, and the money that we'd make from the business would get us a bigger house eventually. His mother owned a four-bedroom townhouse, so it seemed perfect. We'd be even closer so we could help her out when needed, and we wouldn't have to worry about all the overhead expenses of maintaining a home and the expenses of operating the store. We finally decided that we would move in with his mother and open the larger store. The new store was a few miles from the old store and down the street from his mother's house. Within minutes, I could get the kids when they got off the bus. This was another perk to staying with his mom.

I remember hanging up our handmade particle board sign over our store's door. We couldn't afford to have a sign made, so we used what resources we had to make it work. I looked up at that black piece of hand-painted wood with white particle board letters spelling out, PRODIGY, and told God that one day, I wanted to see my name in lights. I had a vision and a dream to succeed.

My passion for business increased. This time around, we incorporated men's clothing, and we even added a room called "The Vintage Room," which consisted of used clothes that were donated to us. This room did very well but not well enough to cover all our new, unexpected expenses. A larger space meant we had to add even more inventory, which led us into contracts with mainstream wholesalers. In the new space, we had more visibility, but with visibility came frequent customers who wanted to see something new every time they came to support. We had a few exceptional customers who were very supportive. Mrs. Marilyn is one unforgettable customer who became like family. She was our neighbor and loved our Vintage Room. She owned a beauty salon next door, and every week, she made it her business to come and patronize our store. She had been in business in that location for over a decade and understood the hardship of owning and operating a business. So, she made it a priority to help us out as much as she could. With all the support that we had, we still couldn't make it work.

We made our rent payments on time, but the pile-up of inventory and operating expenses was overwhelming. This was where our real problems began to set in. I began to do what I knew to do best or what came naturally to me and created a new stream of revenue by hosting Open Mic. Mrs. Marilyn's husband came by on Thursdays and set up the sound equipment for us. He had experience working with sound equipment, and he made sure we were taken care of for Open Mic nights. It was amazing. People from all over Hampton Roads came to express themselves via spoken word, music, and dance. We didn't make much money, but the company of people we had visit on Open Mic nights was amazing. I did all the cooking. My green beans became a staple for Open Mic night. For some weeks, people would come just to enjoy the food. What I loved most about open mic was allowing those in the community to express themselves in a safe, nonjudgmental environment.

One night, a young Hispanic lady stopped by. She was in her early thirties, if I had to guess. She performed a spoken word piece. It was a poem that she had written. After Open Mic was over, I spoke to this young lady, and she revealed that she had been having suicidal ideations. Open Mic allowed her to express herself, and she was no longer contemplating suicide. My heart rejoiced like no other, and at that moment, I realized that God was using me to reach the masses. We saw people who wouldn't step foot inside a church come to our Open Mic, and there, they were ministered to, healed, and set free of their oppressions.

The great idea of convenience also took a quick turn for the worse. It was challenging living in someone else's house with three children. I needed my own space. I didn't want to deal with his family's issues and our issues. So, we moved out of his mother's house and into the back of our store. We had a section set up in the back with a big-screen television and two couches. It was nice and cozy, but trying to hide it from the neighboring business that shared a hallway that led to the shared bathrooms was hard. I often took the kids to his mother's house to take showers. That, too, came to an end after he informed me that his mother didn't want me and my children to take showers at her house. I was a bit confused and hurt, but it didn't deter me. I honestly can't believe she would say anything like that but I rolled with it, and we stopped going to his mom's house to take showers.

My mother-in-law was and has always been very sweet to me and my children. So, after that conversation, I decided that me and the kids would just go to my father's house. He was about fifteen minutes away, and we have always been welcomed to come and go as we pleased. To this day, I still have a key to my parents' house. I washed our clothes at my father's house while my parents were at work. I tried to keep them out of my personal business as much as possible. Not too many people knew we were living out of the store. Besides it being illegal, I was embarrassed. I felt like I had failed again, and more importantly, I had failed my children.

Our finances started getting worse and worse. We borrowed money to keep up with our inventory demands and upgrades to the store. It got out of hand. Eventually, we closed the store with the debt and a new baby. My heart was broken. It felt like a piece of me had died. There were so many thoughts and emotions, many emotions that I had to bury inside and move on. The most important part of business is knowing when to get in and when to get out; this was our time to get out.

Thinking about all the relationships that I had built and bonds that I had made was killing me. There were these three little girls who had followed me down the street to our second location. They would come into the store every day after school, say, "Hi, Mrs. Walker," and buy snacks. I enjoyed seeing them. As the years passed, we grew closer and closer, and they began to share personal things with me. I learned that they were in foster care and lived right behind the store. At every opportunity I had, I mentored them. I grew to love them, and they became a part of me that they may never know. It's been more than seven years, and I still miss them. I wish that I could somehow reconnect with them to see how they are doing.

Soon after, my husband was in a car accident, and our vehicle was totaled. He was leaving the KempsRiver Shopping Center and was hit by a driver who didn't have the right of way. The money we received from the insurance company was used to secure a new home for our family. It wasn't much, but it was ours, and we were glad to be in our own home again. This was a hard lesson learned: home before business. The foundation that you build on must be solid, or everything on top of it will eventually fall.

As time went on, life was better, or at least I seemed that way. The simple arguments we used to have, we no longer had. I learned to love my husband, and I think he loved me too, but love wasn't enough. During this time, the biggest issue was our sex life or lack thereof. It seemed like every time we tried to be intimate, I would be in so much discomfort. I burned uncontrollably, and my desire to be touched went away. He had the usual complaints that most men have, "You never just take it. Why don't you touch me?" I wasn't interested, not because I didn't want to be intimate with my husband, but because it was too much pain for me to bear.

I did everything that I knew to do to resolve the issue. I frequently visited my gynecologist, and after multiple failed attempts to get a diagnosis, I had given up. Our sex life was becoming more and more absent, and we needed a solution fast. He thought it would help if we had a meeting with our pastors. I loved our pastors, and there wasn't anything that I wouldn't share with them. He told our pastors that he thought that I was allergic to him. I will never forget my pastor's response. I was told that it was a spiritual attack and that it was in my head because the doctor couldn't find anything wrong with me.

This was a slap in my face. I knew I wasn't crazy and that it wasn't in my head, so I continued to see my doctor, sometimes visiting him multiple times a month. The most he could do was prescribe me an oral pain medication, an internal medication, and lidocaine. I kept complaining, and the only explanation he could come up with was I was having an allergic reaction to my birth control. So, my doctor decided to remove my birth control to see if that would help. He then placed me on a birth control pill, but I have always been horrible at keeping up with taking pills. I tried for a while, but that didn't help either. I was still having burning sensations. It became so bad that I could not urinate sitting down. I had to stand up and urinate in a cup to keep the urine from touching my skin.

My doctor told me to call him as soon as the symptoms started so he could squeeze me in. He wanted to examine me immediately. So, one day I did that just. I called the doctor's office and told him that I needed to come in. He did the usual vaginal exam. To my surprise, he could see what I was feeling. He said that the inside of my vagina looked like someone had taken a blade and sliced me up. He couldn't believe his eyes. Finally, a diagnosis: Contact Dermatitis. Apparently, it was the soap I had been using that I was allergic to. Every Christmas, my husband's brother would purchase this specific gift and give it to us each year. I chuckled when I connected the dots and discovered why we have years of an irregular sex life. I was also happy that there would be some relief. But there was also a little surprise on the way. We were getting ready to welcome our second child.

Now that the layoffs were over and overtime was available, my husband was working long hours, and he continued to do landscaping on the side. I stayed at home with the kids. My passion for entrepreneurship never left me, so I made his landscaping an official business. I researched and filed the paperwork, and I had business cards, T-shirts, and flyers made. I handled the marketing aspect of the company, and he did the labor. I had so many ideas. Landscaping is such a manual labor job, and I didn't want him out there in the hot sun hustling and bustling. I wanted him to sit back in a cool, air-conditioned truck while he handed out instructions for the day to a crew. He heard me, but his vision didn't seem to line up with mine. I even offered to take classes to secure the licenses we needed for certain jobs; I pictured us having government contracting jobs. Every now and then, if he was behind on a job, I would go out and help him mow the grass. I thought this would be a time that we could spend together. I preferred helping him cut grass over going to work for somebody else making pennies. I saw firsthand the money we made on our own and knew I couldn't make that money working for someone else. In between research and marketing for our landscaping business, I worked a couple of jobs here and there to keep money in my pocket, but depending on him to watch the kids was far harder than financially struggling. My oldest two children and my husband just couldn't get along. Now, I know you're wondering why I desired a job with two incomes coming in, and I will tell you. Although we had two incomes coming in, we didn't share bank accounts, and I had no access to "our" money.

One night, I was working and received a call from my oldest daughter screaming that my husband had dragged my oldest son out of the house. I abruptly left my job to rush home, deal with the police, and try to be the peace maker. I never wanted my children to be in an abusive home, and I didn't want my children to feel like I was choosing anyone over them. I just wanted peace, but it didn't seem that we would experience that any time soon. So, for years, we struggled financially. Our blended family wasn't blending as well as I had envisioned or even believed it to be. We were a mess. Outsiders assumed that everything was going well because we smiled when we needed to, conducted business how we needed to and went to church faithfully and served how we needed to.

CHAPTER SIX
WAR ROOM

WITH EVERYTHING THAT WAS GOING ON AT HOME, the one thing we both agreed to was church. Serving in the church became our lifestyle. In the beginning, I was an armourbearer for my pastor, and I absolutely loved it. I was determined to be the best amour bearer I could be. It required some time away from home, and my husband didn't understand everything that went along with the position. He wanted me to be at home more, and I couldn't hear him because I was too busy serving. Eventually, he, too, became an amour bearer and his complaints of me spending too much time at church went away because he then understood.

Sunday mornings were the absolute worst. As amour bearers, we were expected to be at the church before the pastors arrived to make sure that the air was adjusted to fit the season and everything was ready for ministry. My husband didn't have an issue being on time because he only had to get himself dressed. He would get dressed and leave me to get the four children ready. It frustrated me to no end.

I felt myself resenting him more and more. We would argue about something the night before church and go to bed mad, with me on my side, drowned in tears and he on his side, not uttering a mumbling word. He would get up the next morning and get dressed, all while ignoring me. After I and the children arrived at the church, he'd see me, and it seemed all our problems had magically dissolved, and we were the perfect couple. He had a habit of pulling me to the side after I arrived at church and apologizing. At first, I would accept his apologies and move on like a good Christian wife should, but after a while, it became tiring. We were repeating the same cycle.

I was tired of putting on a show like we were the perfect couple when, in reality, we were broken and simply maintaining. The show became even worse as we became more involved in the church. We were ordained as Deacon and Deaconess. I was a part of the youth ministry, and I also became the church administrator. Our life in the church flourished. I loved serving in the church. It became my new high and took me away from the issues we were having at home.

The hardest part of serving was putting on a mask and pretending that everything at home was okay. I couldn't hide how I was feeling. I received a couple of prophecies during that time that I am thankful for. They showed that despite my service and having to put on a show, I couldn't hide from God or put on a show for God. He knew my pain, and He saw it all. I thought serving in the church was putting God first and that by serving, He would fix all my secret issues. That wasn't the case. I continued to serve, and my issues went unresolved for years. There's a scripture in the Holy Bible that says, "You keep track of all my sorrows. You have collected all my tears in your bottle. You have recorded each one in your book (Psalm 56:8 NLT)". This hit home for me. I knew by now I had a lake of tears. I needed God now more than ever.

In 2015, the movie *War Room* came out in theaters. *War Room* is about a husband and wife, who on the outside, look like they have it all together.

However, their marriage was failing, and the wife, played by Priscilla Shrier, became more and more bitter. She met a lady who encouraged her to turn her closet into a prayer room and to "war" in prayer.

Some time had passed, and we had moved out of our townhouse—the one we got after my husband's car accident. This home was a spacious four-bedroom house in Virginia Beach, Virginia. I will never forget this house because of its unique features, specifically the laundry room. This laundry room was huge. We had the washer and dryer hooked up. A nightstand with a television sitting atop it and two chairs. We placed a cream-colored rug on the floor. I had enough space in this room to feel comfortable for a long time. There was even a window in the laundry room. While I was in the laundry room to wash and fold clothes, I often watched TV.

This room soon became my room of escape. I remember locking myself in the laundry room during a very heated argument with my husband. I used this room to pray. I began to write down my prayers just like in the movie, and day by day, I saw that God was beginning to answer them. This room helped me to maintain my sanity in my not-so-perfect world. One day, I was in my room praying, and I heard God speak to me and say, "If you don't renew your vow, your marriage will not make it." I took heed of what God said to me, and I told my husband and a few mutual friends. I honestly don't think they understood. However, sometime later, my husband confessed his love for me in front of the entire church during a Sunday service. That was as far as that vow renewal went. I was caught off guard when he called me to the front of the church to confess his love for me. I smiled and proceeded like all was well with my husband and me, but internally, I was broken, and his words were merely words with no action or any promise of change. I recall a conversation with someone who was in the service at that time, and she said that she could see the pain all over my face.

Sometime after, I received a phone call from a member of our church. I honestly can't remember why or even how she obtained my phone number, but she called me. I went into the laundry room and closed the door. She began to tell me intimate, untold secrets of my marriage, and tears immediately began to fall down my face. She told me things that nobody but me and God knew. One detail she shared with me is that God showed her a vision of me crying silently in my bed at night. This was the beginning of a long relationship with her because I knew that God had sent her to give me an outlet to vent. I have always been a private person, and if she hadn't told me the intimate details about what was going on in my house the way she did, I would have never opened up to her. God knew just what I needed.

We became very close and began spending a lot of time together. She was one of the people that accompanied me when I viewed *War Room*. I had picked up a seasonal job at Liberty Tax service thanks to my daughter's grandmother, Mrs. Pam. I got off some nights at midnight, and it just so happened that my new friend worked for an insurance agency not too far from my job. After work, we often met at Walmart, and together, we'd purchase our kids' lunch for the week. It was so convenient because there was hardly anyone in the store, which meant no long lines. It wouldn't have mattered anyway because we were killing time. To me, it was more than grocery shopping, and I believe it was much more for her as well. I could laugh and joke and just be me. I had found someone that I could let my guard down with, and whatever was bothering me, I could let it out. These outings were very therapeutic for both of us. On some nights, we even went to the twenty-four-hour McDonald's, off Holland Road, and enjoyed a dollar caramel sundae, cried, talked, and then went home. And some nights, we were out until two or three o'clock in the morning. I wasn't in a rush to get home. My husband and I couldn't get along. He was asleep anyway, and the children were also asleep. Time just seemed to fly. I needed this time to breathe.

CHAPTER SEVEN

MY VISION

FOR YEARS, I TALKED ABOUT PURCHASING A HOUSE, and he was against it, but finally, he agreed. I know what you're thinking, *"How bad could the marriage have been if you were trying to buy a house?"* Well, to answer your question, things were bad, but divorce had never crossed my mind, and I just knew that God was going to fix my marriage. I didn't get married with the intent to walk away.

I got on the phone and went to work. I located a realtor and a mortgage company. During the approval process with the bank, I was the only point of contact. I submitted all the necessary documents. When we received our approval, the realtor began to take both of us out to look at properties. This process was the worst experience ever. It seemed like every house we wanted fell through. We walked around for weeks trying to find the right property. It was like everything we wanted magically disappeared. Eventually, I stumbled across a little house in the Green Run area of Virginia Beach,

VA. It was about one thousand square feet. The pictures of the property showed some additional square footage that had been added to the house but not calculated in the house square footage. I decided that it was worth looking into and scheduling a viewing. Upon arrival, it looked nothing like the house that I had dreamed about or envisioned, but I was determined to see what it had to offer.

As we turned the key, the door opened, and a foul smell hit us directly in the face. It was like something had died in the house. As a matter of fact, the way the house smelled, something must have died in it. Later, we learned that the previous owners had dogs. It was the smell of animal urine that we were smelling. I could barely breathe. Imagine animal urine in a closed house with no air circulating for months; it was horrid. While touring the house, I moved as fast as possible, often having to go outside to get fresh air. The house had been completely destroyed. The floors were ripped up and there laid bare concrete. The previous owners had smashed large holes in the walls. There was graffiti with obscene words throughout, and it was completely unlivable. At the back of the house, there was an attachment that was added to the house. It was almost like an apartment, or in my eyes, it could be a rental property.

Despite what I physically saw, in the spirit, I saw a property that could be built into something beautiful, and I wanted it. I saw an investment. My husband was against it, but after I explained to him that this was just an investment property and that later on, we could go back and get what we really wanted, he agreed that we would purchase the house as an investment property. We put in an offer. The bank approved our offer, and we were on to the next phase. When the numbers came back, I couldn't believe just how much of a return we would get on our investment. After the initial fourteen thousand dollars of repairs, the house would be worth eighty thousand dollars more than what we paid for it. After talking to an experienced investor, we learned that we had to live in the house for two years to avoid the capital gains tax. So, we agreed that we would stay in the house for two years and then sell it. I will never forget the conversation I had with our realtor. He jokingly said, "If I would have known you were going to make that much money off this house, you would have never gotten it." In other words, he was saying he would have purchased the home himself.

At this time, I'm still working my seasonal job at Liberty Tax. It didn't pay much, but I worked as much as I could to help with the closing costs. My goal was to save at least one thousand dollars. My mother gave me a thousand, and my father assisted as well. My husband called on a few of his family members, and they, too, gave as much as they could. I believe everyone was excited for us.

During the repair stage, I hired the general contractor, who was a family friend. I wrote letters to the bank to explain where the allocated funds for repairs would be dispersed and went on to find every contractor that did the work in the house. I chose the wall colors, light fixtures, kitchen cabinets, toilets, doors, doorknobs, and baseboards. I designed the entire house, except for the yellow wall in the kitchen; that was his idea. He also wanted to trim the window in yellow.

We chose a 203k loan with the bank to finance the house. This loan covered the purchase price of the home plus the cost of repairs. The house was a little over thirty years old and was outdated already, so add in the damages from the previous owners, and you'll be able to visualize the needed repair cost. There were a host of repairs that needed to be done. We chose the repairs that had to be done to pass the bank's inspection, and the rest was cosmetics. If you have ever completed a home renovation, then you know that there are always unexpected repairs that come up while you're working on your project. We left a little cushion for that, but it wasn't much.

One of the stipulations for the 203k loan is that the bank issues one check during the middle of the project and the last check after the work has been approved by the bank's inspector. This means that the contractors must front the money for the materials and do not get paid until the project is completed. Our general contractor had materials and laborers to complete his portion of the job. The second contractor we hired for the remaining parts of the job worked privately on the side for himself. He didn't have the financial backing to fund the job in advance, so we had to pay for the materials and his labor upfront. The only reason we agreed to pay him out of pocket was because of his quality work and his prices. He was very reasonable, and his work was spectacular. I am very particular when it comes to presentation, and I wanted the work to look superb. None of this would have been an issue for us if we really had the money to front the project ourselves; however, technically we did not. My husband had a line of credit and credit card with the bank, and we decided that we would use the credit card to purchase the materials, and he would put the money back on his card when the bank cut the final check. The check was issued to my husband because I was not on the loan because of my income and credit at the time of the purchase. It really wasn't important to me because we were married, and the house would legally be mine because of state law. The money was never applied to the credit card once we received the final check for the repair reimbursement, so our debt began to pile up. Five thousand dollars for the floors were charged to the credit card. Every day, it was something different that had to be paid for, and he charged it to his credit card, without my consent.

Finally, it's move-in day. We couldn't get all the work done that we would have wanted to complete, but the house was livable. I called in a few favors and worked out a few deals to get a few extra things done. It looked like a totally new house. My mom had given me money to get a few things to decorate the house, and things were slowly coming together.

A few weeks later, I threw a housewarming party. We had a house full of people who came to support us in the purchase of our new home.

There were so many people in the house that the air conditioner stopped working properly. It couldn't produce enough cool air to keep the house cool. Everyone was there except my husband. He decided that he would work and cut grass instead. I understand that our money was tight, and we needed all the extra that we could get, but this was a very special occasion that he knew about in advance before he decided to schedule a job. I was livid! We didn't look like a united front, and we were by far not a united front.

My most unforgettable memory of the day was my aunt, Angel, spending the day with me to help prepare the food. I never had anyone take the time to teach me how to cook until this day. My biological mom didn't cook much. She said my great-grandmother didn't teach her how to cook because she would eat while she was cooking, and Grandma didn't like that.

Months passed, and the excitement of home ownership vanished. What was supposed to be a home was just a house. We were back to the basics, simply existing together. He continued to work from dawn to dusk, and we continued to serve in church as usual. Although I loved serving at my church, it became an issue for me when I noticed that my husband would kill himself—figuratively speaking—to do whatever our pastors asked him to. If I asked him to do something, it was met with resistance.

Our schedules didn't vary from week to week. It was the exact same schedule, and I became bored. There was no excitement, no change. Just the same old routine. On Mondays and Tuesdays, he'd come home at night, take his shower, eat, and go to bed. Any spare time that he had was spent streaming TV on his phone. He never wanted to go anywhere, and he was always too tired to entertain me or the kids. Wednesday night was Bible study. From work, he'd rush home, and off we went to church, no matter how tired he was. Occasionally, on Saturdays, we'd meetings or other church functions, and of course, there were Sundays. Sundays started early with leadership meetings, intercessory prayer, and then the worship service.

After service, the deacons and deaconesses all cleaned the sanctuary of a five thousand-square-foot building. After service, there were also meetings for specific ministries. It was a lot and overwhelming at times, but I truly loved it. I just didn't love how we spent so much time at church and we did nothing to keep our marriage fresh and alive.

The only time we really did anything as far as going on a date was when the church had marriage ministry outings. Those were the absolute best. We would go and be refueled, only to go home and practice nothing that we had learned. Our pastors would even invite the amor bearers and their spouses out to eat after church on Sundays. I used to love being able to have that one-on-one time with them and really loved when my husband would go with me. But most of the time, I went alone. It didn't cost us a dime to go. Our pastors paid most of the time unless the amour bearers pulled together and paid for their food to be a blessing to them. Them covering our bill wasn't even enough to make him want to go out, so money could not have been the issue. I begged my husband for years to "date me again." I needed more of him, and I had no desire to seek attention from anyone else. I was faithful to my husband and had eyes for him only. I loved him.

My husband was known in the church for being very encouraging, and it was said that he had the gift of encouragement. He would send text messages with encouraging messages to members of the church, and I would often get told about the messages. I would smile and nod when they praised him. On the inside, I was burning up because that was not the man that I lived with. One member even recommended that he establish a separate Facebook page to encourage others. That later became part of the demise of our marriage. You'll learn why later in the book.

He often said that I didn't appreciate him. I'm sure many of you are familiar with Gary Chapman's book, *The 5 Love Languages*. After learning that my husband's top love language was words of affirmation, I understood why he would say that. It wasn't that I didn't appreciate him; it was the fact that I had such a great dad. He worked long days and nights, took care of two households, had his own issues, and still was emotionally available to me. I did appreciate my husband. In my mind, cleaning and taking care of the house and kids was my way of showing him I appreciated him. Being faithful and taking his mess was my way of appreciating him. I often told him that he was a hard person to love, and God knows he was very hard for me to love him.

My top two love languages are physical touch and quality time. I would try to physically touch him and spend time with him, but I didn't feel like he appreciated that. But then, those weren't his love languages. In hindsight, I should have verbally expressed that I appreciated him more. Maybe he would have felt that I did. He wasn't the most affectionate person, and we didn't spend any time together. Looking back, it all just seems like miscommunication or a lack of communication between two people who really loved each other but didn't know how to express it. My heart's desire was for him to show me he loved me through physical touch and quality time. We didn't take the time to really discover each other's love languages.

It didn't bother him if we ever cuddled or held hands. I recall years of desiring what we had at the beginning of our relationship. In the beginning, we held hands. I have a habit of holding the gearshift when I drive; it makes me feel like I'm on the racetrack. He would take his hand and place it over mine while I drove. That faded, and honestly, I'm not sure when it faded or why. Maybe the excitement of a new relationship was gone, and we were just existing. During our entire eight-year marriage, we visited our families, but I wouldn't consider that time spent on us to develop our marriage. If I separate the family visits, I can say that we went on two vacations. This is solely based on the distance of the trips and the kids not being present. One was a business trip that I planned to Vegas, and the second was a trip that we took to Spotsylvania, Virginia. The reason why we went on that trip was because his aunt had rented a cabin for her birthday for a week, and she couldn't go as early as she had planned. So she called us and asked if we wanted to go, so we went.

I thought that this would be an amazing opportunity for us to have a break from the kids and really enjoy ourselves; it started out that way. We ate at a Japanese steak house the first night. It was my first time, and I really enjoyed it. Later, we went food shopping for shrimp, and then we went to Dollar General and purchased steaks, seasonings, snacks, eggs, and turkey bacon. It was fun to see how much money we could save when only feeding two people. We made the best with what we had and enjoyed just being responsible for us.

The next night in the cabin, I cooked the steak and shrimp. We indulged in a bottle of liquor; this was the first time that we had ever drank an alcoholic beverage together. After our meal, we played strip poker. I was thinking, *we are about to get it in!* I was excited! There are no children and no interruptions to worry about. We became intimate. In the middle of our lovemaking, I told him something that I wanted him to do to me that would bring me more pleasure. He jumped up and went downstairs. I didn't bother to go after him. We had been drinking alcohol, and I was exhausted. It was late, and I thought that he was going to come back up the stairs. He did not!

The next morning, I asked him why he stopped having intercourse with me and walked downstairs, and he said, "You cheated on me." I thought his statement was hilarious because I had never cheated on him. I was simply exploring my sexual desires with my husband. For my husband to believe that I cheated on him because I asked him to do something different sexually floored me. This was supposed to be the safe place, right? I am a very vocal person. I don't have an issue expressing myself and saying what I want and what I need. Throughout my marriage, I consistently told him what I needed; it just wasn't received or processed. At that very moment, I knew that my routine marriage and sex life was going to continue to be routine, and I'd have to live with it, and for a few years, that is exactly how we lived. This confirmed to me that I couldn't express myself to my husband and be completely free with him.

CHAPTER EIGHT
FINDING ME

YEARS PASSED, AND NOTHING HAD CHANGED IN MY MARRIAGE. I become frustrated with juggling my emotions and desiring attention and affection from my husband. The disrespect and inconsideration were taking a toll on me. Everything that I had suppressed for years was coming out. I went back and forth with myself about how I was going to proceed with my marriage. I knew that if I was going to walk away, I needed a solid source of income.

I decided to create a new business in my name only. At that time, all I could think about was how all of our other businesses were in his name and how he had the final say on what happened to them, no matter how much capital or sweat equity I invested. I needed my voice back. I needed my independence back. More importantly, I needed to know what Latoria Danielle could do!

There were so many occasions when he would tell me that I couldn't do this or that without him. He knew my credit was jacked up and that I needed him, or at least, he thought I needed him. Repairing my credit was the second part of finding myself. My biggest hindrance was my defaulted student loans. I was honestly afraid to contact the creditors. I had stayed off the radar for so long because I was working in our family business, and we used his credit for everything. What I didn't want was for them to garnish his wages to pay back my student loans. I didn't think that was fair to him, given that I had acquired them before we met. One day, I conjured up enough courage to call the student loan company. I set up a payment plan to get my student loans out of default, and when the default was lifted, my loans appeared on my credit report in good standing. My credit score jumped up!

My "late-night hangout partner" from earlier became my motivational partner. Her goal was to be a homeowner, and I just wanted to better myself. We both downloaded a credit monitoring app. And together, we shared different information to help us increase our credit score. We both obtained secured credit cards through our bank. This is a really good way to help give your credit a boost. We were on to something. As the weeks went by, we would share our victories no matter the size of the increase.

Christmas was around the corner, and like every year, we waited until the last minute to buy the kids Christmas stuff. He gave me what money he could, but it wasn't enough for me. My parents had painted this image in my head of the floor being covered with presents on Christmas morning. My anxiety was kicking in, and all I could think of was my kids being as happy as I was as a child on Christmas day.

One day, I talked to my friend, and she told me about this company that does in-house financing. After concluding our conversation, I thought this would be a great idea because they reported the payments to the credit bureau. I could get more stuff for the kids, and I could get a boost to my credit score for on-time payments. A few days later, my husband and I decided to check the store out. It was an electronic store, and our oldest son was the only one who really didn't have many gifts. I thought getting him a game system would be great.

When we arrived at the store, I was told that to finance the game system, I had to purchase a TV. So, we agreed to get a TV that was large enough for our living room wall. With the additional expense of the TV, there was no way that I could afford to make the monthly payment each month. My husband assured me that he would help. As expected, my income wasn't reliable, and it came to where I could no longer make the payments. My husband agreed to make the payments. Everything was going well, then suddenly, he decided he wasn't going to make the payments anymore. I couldn't afford to make the payments, so of course, this impacted my credit negatively. This was the second time that he had done this to me, so I shouldn't have been alarmed. The first time was when he convinced me to put the cable in my name. What had baffled me the most was he always paid his bills on time. His agreeing to pay my bills and then deciding not to almost seemed like it was a setup to keep me down. Well, at least, that's how it made me feel.

Later that year, my friend bought her house! A single mother with nothing but determination. She did it, and I was so proud of her. For months, she battled whether it would happen. Together, we prayed and cried, and she did it. She motivated me even more now. Her strength is remarkable even when she doesn't know it.

So now it is tax season. I knew that I was making my escape plan, so I decided to file my taxes on my own without my husband. I knew that this would give me the financial break that I needed. I filed my taxes without my husband and was able to get a seven thousand dollar refund. I decided that it was my turn to step out on faith. I signed the lease in my business's name on a small commercial space to operate my new coaching business and my non-profit business. The rent was cheap, and the utilities were included. I had run it by my husband earlier in the year, and he dismissed it. I was still desiring his approval, but after I was shot down, I kept moving with my vision. It wasn't much, but I had a window and a private entrance. I scrapped together what money I had and bought a desk, office chair, and couch for my clients. I took a few decorations from our house that my mom had given me to put on the wall in my office, and I was in business.

I had a few business items at the house in our garage that were heavy, so I had a male family friend come to my home to pick them up and deliver them to my office. My husband was infuriated that I had a man in our home. To this day, I have no idea how he figured out that a man had helped me. For the second time, I was accused of cheating, but of course, I wasn't. Honestly, I don't think that he really thought I was cheating, but he was more upset that I was making moves without him. I had depended on him for everything for so long, and now, I no longer needed him. I won't say it was easy, but I had to do what I needed to do to get back on my feet. Any and every resource that I could use, I used. I purchased my desk at Office Max. They loaded the desk in my car, but I couldn't get it out. I had to get help with that too. This was a new transition for me, but I thank God for the friends who supported me to make sure that I was taken care of. When I opened my office, my husband didn't step inside. The closest he got was in the parking lot to pick up our kids. It didn't bother me; I had my independence, and that's all I really cared about.

Our marriage was rockier than ever. My church attendance decreased, but my business was thriving. I had enough clientele to cover my overhead and even had enough to live off. I had always gotten in trouble in school for talking, and now, people were paying me to talk to them, to talk about something that I loved dearly—entrepreneurship. My student loan debt and all the money I had invested in books and business was finally paying off for itself, and it felt good. I felt on top of the world.

During this time, I had also made a contractual agreement with a local restaurant to host Open Mic on Tuesday nights. It was almost as if God was giving me back everything that I had lost. It was much different than when I hosted back in the early 2000s at our boutique because this was a more secular setting. Each week, I would go out to buy a different outfit. My goal was to find an outfit under five dollars, and most weeks, I was successful. It felt good to be able to buy something for myself instead of receiving hand-me-downs. Sometimes, the clothes wouldn't be my style or my true size, but I worked it out, and you would never know. I am tremendously thankful for friends and family who gave me clothes when I needed them, but it felt good to purchase clothes for myself. My focus for so long had been on my home and making sure that the kids had what they needed. It was so bad when I started shopping that I didn't even know what size I was. I had to try many different sizes and pieces to determine the right size.

It reminded me of going shopping with my mother. We would be in Belk's or JCPenney's for hours, and after finding a few things she liked and trying them on, she would return them all back to the racks because she didn't like how they fit. I hated going shopping with her, and now, I understood how it felt to have to try on clothes and figure out what fit your body type. I could see my mother all in me. Now, I am the one in the store for hours, walking out with nothing. Before opening my office, our family business profits went back into the business and had only covered minor things that were needed. I had forgotten about what I liked and what I needed. Wearing a new outfit made me look forward to hosting Open Mic Nights, even with my nerves through the roof. I wanted to look the part, and looking the part made me feel like I was being paid one million dollars each Tuesday.

I was responsible for hosting and generating revenue for the establishment through food and alcohol sales. Some nights, we would have a good turnout; other nights, not so good, but I made some lifelong relationships.

On the stage, I was free. When it was slow, I had to perform, and I was really stepping out of my comfort zone. But the more I did it, the more comfortable and easier it became. Freedom rang louder than ever, and the fear of not being able to sing went out the window. I'm no Whitney Houston, but I sound good! I had a passion for singing when I was growing up. My cousin and I wrote songs and sang all the time. After years of others saying that I couldn't sing and that I sing out of my nose, I began to believe them. One Tuesday night, there was a guy who owned a recording studio in Virginia Beach in the audience. He offered to allow me to use his studio for free anytime. I never took him up on his offer, but hopefully, when I'm ready, the offer will still be on the table. I still desire to make a record, even if I'm only a one-hit wonder. It's on my bucket list. I even had a poet ask me why I was singing in the lounge and not on a big stage. I don't know if I'll make it to the big stage, but don't be surprised if I do!

CHAPTER NINE

THE FINAL STRAW

ONE AFTERNOON, AROUND 3:30 P.M., I WAS SITTING IN THE living room, watching TV, when my husband walked in the door from work. I greeted him. Without making any eye contact, he walked past me as if he didn't hear or see me. I stood up and followed him to the refrigerator. Our open floor plan, one-thousand-square-foot home was very cozy, and there was no way he didn't hear me. I repeated myself, "Hello, how was work?" Again, he ignored me. Before I could catch myself, I was blurting out, "This will be the last time that you will ever ignore me." This was the straw that broke the camel's back. I was done! He walked into the master bedroom and locked the door.

He had a habit of ignoring me. It made my flesh cringe, and anger overtook me. At the beginning of our relationship, when he used to ignore me, my heart would break into a million pieces, and my self-esteem felt like it was plummeting to the bottom of the Pacific Ocean. As time progressed, my pain turned into me being equally as disrespectful to him. I was so used to receiving attention from my parents and even random men in the streets who would try to talk to me consistently, and here I was, chasing attention and validation from the man who asked me to marry him. When I wasn't working, I made sure that the house was clean, the kids were taken care of, and that he had a hot meal prepared. I prided myself on making sure that he was taken care of. My parents had me in their later years of life. I grew up "old school," so to speak, and I did exactly what I saw. My father worked, and my mother took care of the house. My mother worked a full-time job just like my father, but she made sure that his food was on the stove when he got home. I never saw my father clean or do any work inside the house except for maintenance things such as fixing the sink or toilet.

When it came to my husband, I knew just when to put the food on the stove. I wanted to make sure that as soon as he turned the doorknob to enter the house, the aroma would hit him in the face. I would lay his clothes out for him. I would even give this man pedicures; I treated him like a king. He might have worked hard outside the home, but when he got home, there wasn't anything for him to do inside the house. I cooked every meal that was made inside of our home because he couldn't cook. I fixed his plate and served him every time he ate. Not to say that there weren't times that he didn't serve himself, but most times, I did it. I loved doing it until I realized that he didn't appreciate it. It was almost like he expected me to do it. At that point, it was a task instead of a love offering from me. I began to hate serving his plates and making his drinks. One day, he even dared to say to me, "You know when you serve someone a plate, you are supposed to give them a drink?" I felt like he had just snatched the breath out of my body. I had slaved over a hot stove and served five plates, and he was asking for something to drink! I hadn't even had the opportunity to make my own plate, which was the sixth plate that had to be fixed. Of course, I was going to fix him a drink as well as everyone else in the house, but I was only one person with two hands. This became the norm; before I could fix my plate, he was asking for seconds. I felt degraded and less of a woman. I never had the desire to be a stay-at-home wife and mother. I enjoyed working. And his final decision to close our 3rd and last store left me in a very depressed space. So, I focused on what I knew to do take care of my husband and house. I was taught to serve my husband, and God would honor that. I was actively doing what I thought would keep my marriage.

There was a time in our marriage, and I do mean a long time as in years when I would sit by the window and wait for him to come home, just as I had done my father as a young child. I could tell by the way the sun was setting that he would be arriving soon. I did this for a countless number of years, but as the marriage began to sink, I dreaded him coming home. As soon as I heard the exhaust from his work truck backing in the yard, I became immediately irritated.

I hated repeating myself and begging him to love me how I needed to be loved; after all, love was something that my father had given me so effortlessly. I didn't understand how he didn't understand my cry for help, especially after I vocalized the same thing over and over for years. Swallowing my tears and repeating the same old cycle time and time again. No matter how I tried to focus on being honorable to God by serving my husband, I couldn't let go of my inner desires to be loved. His working and paying the bills had nothing to do with what I physically and emotionally needed from him. I don't remember the occasion, but he had brought me a yellow rose early on in our relationship while we were dating. No man had ever brought me flowers before, but I liked the feeling that I had when he gave it to me. I wanted the feeling again because it felt good. Throughout our marriage, I said things to my husband like, "I like flowers. It would be nice to have some flowers." I didn't get flowers again until 7 years later for my thirtieth birthday. I recall looking at the flowers, and they were nice, but I had spent seven years begging him for them, and at this point, my investment to get them outweighed their worth, and my value on the flowers had depreciated lower than the value of a brand-new car rolling off the lot with its new owner. I had become numb! They were now just flowers, something that grew every day with no meaning.

My husband ignoring me that day gave me the ammunition to break free. I no longer wanted to feel like I was somewhere that I wasn't wanted, needed, or appreciated. So, I did what most successful married couples would say not to do, and I moved out of our master bedroom. I waited until the next day while my husband was at work, and I moved all of my belongings out of our bedroom into our son's room.

After I moved out of our bedroom, I slept on the couch. The youngest of my kids, who was four years old at the time, would always manage to find his way beside me. There wasn't much room on the couch, but it felt good to have him beside me, so I never complained. Some nights, I would wake up to two more of my children beside me on the floor. It was comforting to know they wanted to be near me, but them seeing me on the couch had to raise red flags for them, even if they didn't understand all that was going on between me and their father. I tried to make things as peaceful as I could for the kids while trying to hold myself together. I didn't want them on the floor, so we all migrated into my fourteen- and four-year-old's room. In this room, there was a queen sized-bed that made the perfect space for the four of us. My seven-year-old daughter would fight with my four-year-old son over who got to sleep beside mommy, so eventually, I decided that I would sleep in the middle of the two of them while my oldest son slept across the bottom of the bed. This wasn't the best sleeping arrangement, but we were all together. It became a game for the kids. It was fun to sleep with mommy. Mommy enjoyed sleeping with the kids. I had slept in the bed with my mom at my double-digit age, so it was all normal for me growing up. The difference was nobody was in my house but me and my mom. And there wasn't any drama that made me feel I needed to sleep with her. I had my own room, but I just preferred being with her. It was difficult sleeping with three children some nights due to the wild sleepers, and of course, I got frustrated because of all of the tossing and turning, but all in all, we had each other. I slept better next to them, and they slept better next to me. This is where I found a piece of peace to keep me going. I went back and forth from their room to the couch some nights just to try and get a few uninterrupted hours of rest. This continued until one night after coming home late; I went to lay down on the couch, and it was soaking wet. At first, I thought that maybe our youngest son had urinated on the couch, but the entire couch was soaked. I quickly eliminated that thought because it wasn't wet in one spot. Then it dawned on me. My husband had poured water on the couch because he was angry at me. This would be the beginning of a very abusive, toxic end. The wet couch didn't deter me; it just added to why I needed to get away from him. As petty as it was and as much as I wanted to retaliate, I did not. I simply moved my purse and blankets inside my daughter's room and slept there for the night.

There were countless times that I thought about getting back at him for the stuff that he did to me, but all I could think about was him having a case against me and me losing my children. I couldn't imagine not having them, and they honestly kept me safer than they'll ever really know.

As crazy as it might sound, my husband was trying to save our marriage the best way he knew how I guess. In one of our conversations, he said to me if he had known that buying me flowers would have saved our marriage that he would have brought me flowers every day. All I could feel was hate. His way of getting me back for not wanting to be with him was by doing mean stuff to me, and it was not working at all. I told him over and over, "You win more bees with honey than vinegar." He didn't get it. It went right over his head just like all the other things that I had said to him throughout our marriage. My issues with my husband and our marriage were deeply rooted. In the beginning, I loved the idea of getting flowers, but after a while, I really didn't want the flowers. Towards the end, I needed him to buy the flowers so that I knew he heard me. Looking back at the situation, I was extremely angry and hurt at how he had treated me over the years.

During a domestic situation with my oldest two children and my husband at our home, the police were called to our house as well as our pastors. After the matter was resolved with the police, our pastors stayed back to talk to us. They were trying all that they knew to do to help us save our marriage, but I was over it. How could I possibly be with a man who clearly had an issue with the children that I brought to the marriage? I know the Christian model is God first, husband, wife, then children. In a normal family scenario, I can agree with this; however, putting a man before my children who was mistreating them is crazy. During this visit, my pastors asked him to give me a hug. He got up to hug me, and as he got up and walked towards me, I said to myself that this man hadn't touched me in months. I just sat there with my arms in my lap in disgust. He was clearly hurt, but we had been down this road before, and the same thing kept recurring. I felt like I deserved more; my children deserved more, and we deserved more than what he had shown me he was willing to give. After 8 years of someone not getting it right, I wasn't willing to waste another moment of my life doing the same exact thing. I didn't know what would change our situation, and I kept telling him that I needed some time to myself and wanted to be alone. We had met with the pastors throughout our marriage, and things would change for a couple of days, and we'd go right back to doing the same thing. We had done this for eight years, and the issues were still the same. I was told I was being selfish, but deep down,

I knew that I wasn't being selfish, and in all actuality, not putting myself first or even considering what I wanted for my life was what had brought me to this point in my life. I had stayed with him after he intentionally got me pregnant without my consent. I stayed with him because it was his first child and I wanted to give my children a full family experience. I had already made sacrifices for everyone else and not considered myself. I was tired of hearing scriptures and getting spiritual advice; I was burnt out.

A mutual friend of ours had told her mother about what was going on, and she gave me a call. It was easy to talk to her, and I felt like she was one of the only people to understand where I was. Her approach was more about my mental stability and me getting the help I needed. It was understood that I loved God and that I knew the word of God. I gave my life to God on my own at the age of 8. I remember that service like it was yesterday. I told God that all I wanted was to be closer to Him, and that has been the story of my entire life—to get to know Him more intimately. Sadly, my belief in Christianity was questioned during this time and still is. I had posted a picture of me on Facebook, and I was told that I looked like I was possessed by a demon. None of this was true. I was finally seeing the light and was breaking away from the grain. I have never been one to follow the crowd, and I have always been one to make my own way. It's like it's in my DNA, and I can't shake it.

The tension in the house began to grow even thicker. We weren't speaking to each other. He even stopped eating my food. One day, I was in the living room doing my daughter's hair, and my husband walked into the house. He didn't speak and just asked for my car keys. This was a car that he had purchased for me as a gift because he had totaled my Mercedes. I told him that I wasn't giving him my keys. I asked him what he needed with my car, and he said that he needed our son's car seat. I told him that I would get the car seat for him. I reached behind my back to get the keys. I got up from the couch and walked towards the door. He grabbed my arm to take the keys out of my hand. We physically struggled for a while but eventually, I gave up because the bracelets that I had on my arm were cutting into my skin. I released the keys and immediately slapped him in the neck. That's all that I could reach because he is much taller than me. He walked outside, got whatever he needed out of the car, and then he came back into the house. He put my keys on the counter and left. Later that week, a sheriff was knocking on my door handing me a summon to go to court. My husband went down to the magistrate's office and placed a proactive order against me. He told the police that he was in fear for his life. I was devastated. I couldn't believe that he would make a false report on me.

This crazy roller-coaster continued. I wasn't sure what was happening, but everything was spiraling out of control, and I needed it all to stop because it was happening too fast. I was desperate to make it all stop, so I decided to talk to my husband about fixing our marriage. After all the praying he was doing and all the phone calls he had made to our family members, trying to get them to talk me into staying, he had now decided that he no longer wanted to be married. For weeks, I literally begged my husband to fix our marriage against my better judgment. I stopped coming in late and was spending more time in the house like I used to. Not being home became my way of dealing with what was happening at home. My feelings hadn't changed about wanting to be with him. I didn't love him and no longer desired to be with him. My decision to fix the marriage was to save my family and to continue with the original goal and that was to ensure that my children had a two-parent home. He shot me down every time. I couldn't understand what was happening. It seemed like every time I would try to fix the marriage, God blocked it. I was still trying to seek God on what was happening. All I know is that I needed to make sure that I was making the best decision possible concerning my children.

Our toxic relation was our new normal, and I became used to it, but what I wasn't used to was the police being called back and forth to my home and my children suffering the way they were suffering. I needed all of it to stop. My final attempt to fix my marriage was when I decided that I was going to move back into the marital bedroom. My husband was out late one night, and when he returned home, to his surprise, I was in our room on our bed. He asked me to leave the room, and I refused. After a few minutes of arguing about me being in the room, he decided that he would flip the mattress over with me on it. I jumped off when I realized what he was doing, but our then preschooler son was still on the bed. He didn't get hurt, but he could have. I became very irritated, picked up a dresser drawer, and threw it on the ground. He kept telling me to get out, and I continued to refuse to do so because this was our room in our house, and he couldn't lock me out of any part of our house. He then walked over to me, grabbed me, and pushed me behind our bedroom door.

Behind our bedroom door was a small space in the shape of a square. He then proceeded to hold the door so that I couldn't get out. To get out, I had to scream out to my oldest daughter and ask her to call the police. When she called the police, he ran out of the house. The police arrived at our house shortly after the call, but he was nowhere to be found. He had jumped in the car that he had brought me and fled the scene. They wanted me to press charges, but after all that he had done to me, I still couldn't see myself hurting him. He had a prior criminal record, and I just couldn't do it. I told the officers that I would go to the courthouse and file a protective order against him, but I didn't. This is where I messed up. I didn't protect myself or my children. Keep in mind that he had recently filed for a protective order against me, and I had received my summons to go to court. Things just kept going downhill faster, and I couldn't brace myself for any of what was to come. After the police left, I was outside on the phone telling someone what had happened, and my husband returned to our home on foot. He honestly startled me, and I was afraid because I didn't know what to expect from him. Thankfully, he didn't say anything to me. He just walked past me. What I didn't know was that I wouldn't have possession of my car again after that night. I ended up getting a rental car for a week, and then my dad gave me one of his vehicles so that I could get around. This man even went so far as to cut my cell phone off. My husband would taunt me by bringing the car home every few weeks.

Enough was enough. I found a lawyer immediately and filed for divorce. A few weeks later, it was time to go to court for the protective order that he had filed against me. I had never been in any legal trouble, and he knew that. The fact that he would even go so far as to make this report was hurtful to my core. I felt like he was purposely trying to destroy me. The day we went to court for the Protective Order, I had him served with the divorce papers. He looked like he was in disbelief. I don't know much about getting in trouble with the law, but what I do know is you better have a lawyer and a darn good one. He wasn't expecting me to show up at court with a lawyer. Now, I have money because I was running my business, and I still have my income tax money. After all the evidence was heard, the case was dismissed. The judge said that my husband couldn't be the aggressor and be the victim at the same time. 6 years earlier in our marriage, my husband had physically abused me. He pushed me into a 2nd-floor window. After he pushed me, I hit him. After I hit him for pushing me, he pushed me again. When he pushed me the second time, he pushed me so hard that I lost my balance and hit my head on the footboard of our bed, and I lost consciousness. The fight didn't last long after that, but it took me a while to gain my balance and get back up. The only reason why I am revisiting that issue is to show that my intent was never to hurt him. If I was out to get him, that's when I would have got him. I could have called the police, but I didn't. It never even crossed my mind. The only people that knew about this situation were our pastors because he felt guilty and wanted to talk to our pastors about what happened.

I don't wish divorce on my worst enemy. Not because I care about the enemy but because I care about the people who are connected to the marriage that get hurt in the crossfire. My husband's final attempt to save our marriage was to see a professional marriage counselor. I was against that because I didn't want to talk to anyone about fixing the marriage. The majority of the people that I had talked to about the situation all kept the conversation at "fixing the marriage". I didn't want to hear that, and I just wanted to be left alone. I was overhearing about the marriage and only wanted to hear about me and how to make me better. I wanted to be whole again. I knew that I was broken. After eight years of doing what was best for the family, it was now "me" time. I declined marriage counseling but decided to see the counselor on my own. During our sessions, we talked about me, and I was able to express myself in a safe, unjudgmental setting. The counselor was a neutral party, and I needed help. I decided that I would put all my cards on the table, and I told her everything. My transparency and vulnerability are what allowed me to get the help that I needed. We were able to get to the root of my internal issues and the root issues of my marriage. During one of my sessions, the counselor said that she didn't even know how we had made it 8 years because we didn't even know each other, but I knew the reasoning for that. Rushing a marriage because of a baby and being consumed by work, businesses, and church. We eventually ended up having a group session, but that too didn't go well because, for the first time in 8 years, I was completely honest with myself and my husband. I told my husband that I didn't love him, and I felt like he intentionally got me pregnant to force me to be with him. After the session, I guess he realized that there was no saving the marriage. He began coming home late and some nights not coming home at all. My children were devastated. Some days would go by, and they wouldn't see their father. I know that they could feel all the animosity between us because they began to ask questions that I couldn't answer like, "Why isn't Daddy coming home?" Every time my children asked where their father was, another piece of my heart broke away.

One night, my husband didn't come home, and I decided to go looking for him around 5 am. I went by his mom's house, and I went by a mutual friend's house, whom I thought he may be at. His truck was nowhere to be found. I never mentioned it to him, but I knew something wasn't right, and I needed to find out what. He eventually came home, but when he came home, it was late, and he was very tired. It really wasn't a reason to even question him because I knew that he would only ignore me. So that night, I realized that I had left my charger at my office and needed to charge my phone. I asked him if I could use his charger and he was nice enough to say yes. After my phone charged, I took his charger back to his room to put his phone on the charger. As I was walking to the bedroom door, I could hear him snoring, so I didn't knock on the door to announce my entry. I just walk in. I plugged the charger into the wall outlet and proceeded to grab his cellphone. While I was putting his cellphone on his charger, something within me told me to take his phone and look through it. Now, this was something that I had never done before. Before this situation, I had never had a reason to question my husband, and we both had the liberty and freedom to just go. I never question his whereabouts. So, as I was going through his phone, I was not sure what to look for. I noticed a text message from a female that I had never heard of before, and he was telling her that he was sick, and her response was basically, "Aww I had to work." It seemed innocent, but I took pictures of the text message anyway. I found pictures of two females. One of the pictures looked as if it was old. It appeared that he had taken a picture of an older picture and had it stored in his phone. The second picture was a woman who was dressed in a provocative two-piece outfit. Again, none of this alarmed me. I just continued to take pictures of what I saw. What did however alarm me was pictures inside of his phone of two comedy show tickets that he had purchased but wasn't buying food to put in our house. I took pictures of that too. He had pictures of my credit cards and social security card. I deleted those. At this point, I was in watch mode.

Sometime later, I was having a conversation with my two younger kids, and my youngest daughter told me that they were in my car. Well, she said that they left the house in their dad's truck, and then their daddy blindfolded them with a sock. After their dad blind folded them with a sock, they got out of his truck and got into another vehicle. After the vehicle started moving, their dad instructed them to remove the sock from their eyes. My youngest daughter told me that when she was able to see, they were in my car. She said that their daddy said it was a game. I was outraged! I knew no one would believe me, so I recorded my children telling me the story. At this point, everything had to be documented for my protection. I was in fear for my life and felt like he was going to hurt me because he couldn't get his way. He used materialistic things to control me, and I wasn't allowing that to stop me. I was determined to make it on my own without him. More now than ever, I needed my new business to succeed. I needed to get out of that house, but my lawyer had advised me not to remove the children from the marital property. I ended up putting all my children in one room, and we slept in a queen sized-bed together. I put the dresser to the door, just in case he tried to come in the room so I could hear him. I began to send emails to my pastors as well as a close relative to let them know that I was in fear for my life, and if something happened to me, he was the suspect. My parents were also afraid that he would hurt me if I didn't get out of the house.

CHAPTER TEN

NO ANGEL

I MUST ADMIT DURING MY TRANSITION OF FINDING MYSELF, I was no angel, and I would never tell my story as though I was. What made me stand apart from my husband was that I always told my wrongs. I never wanted anyone to be able to tell my story, and this is one of the many reasons that I chose to write this book. If I had to describe or sum up what my spiritual life was life during the last 6 years of my marriage, I would say that it was borderline perfect. If God had come back for me, I would have had a one-way plane ticket in first class straight to heaven. I was in church almost every time the doors opened. I served God wholeheartedly and had a sincere love for God's people, and it showed throughout my life and servanthood. This wasn't something that could be taught this was spiritually led by God. Something that He had given me that had become my purpose and reason for living. I will be forever grateful to Him for using me how He did and how He will continue to do so. I was studying my bible, fasting, wining souls for Christ, teaching the word of God, prophesying, laying hands, sowing my tithes, and giving back to my community. If it was building the kingdom of God, I was doing it. The only thing I could not shake was cussing. Now I prayed, and yes, I did become more disciplined, but Lord knows it's something I couldn't shake. Every now and then, something was bound to slip out. And let sin number two, anger, not come out. I said all that to say I lived a model life with a couple of sins I couldn't shake. How could I forget I still loved Trap Music? Sin number three, I guess. With my mind, body, and soul sold out for Jesus, I ended up having an affair with another man. I hated my husband for it. I hated him for making me feel like I needed to run to another man to feel the love, comfort, and attention that I wanted from him. No, it wasn't right. I'm not saying that it was. What I am saying is that if my husband had listened to me and paid attention to my actions and understood that all I wanted was for him to love me and how I needed to be loved, no man would have ever had the opportunity to take his place.

My heart was heavier than anyone will ever be able to imagine, but I have forgiven myself and I am free. When my husband caught wind of my affair, he told me that I would reap what I sowed. All I could think about was wanting to reap all that I had sowed because, for many years, I was selfless and had given all that I had to everyone else. I am not perfect. Yes, I committed adultery, but I know surely that after all that I have done in the Kingdom, after all of God's promises to me and my relationship with Him, He would not remove His mighty hand from my life. His Grace and mercy covered me. People are always offended when people say, "God knows my heart". Well, God knew my heart, and my intentions were never to hurt my husband. I was running from pain, hurt, loneness, brokenness, low self-esteem, and confusion, and I needed help! Where I landed may not have been godly, but I found myself in whatever untraditional way God was allowing my life to go. I wouldn't change anything except for how I left. I believe that due to the foundation our marriage was built on—my immaturity and my husband's inability to understand the women that I had grown into and his own demons—our marriage would have failed anyway.

At the beginning of our separation, when I told my husband that I no longer wanted to be married and just wanted my space, that was exactly what I wanted. I was not seeing another man. I needed time to clear my head and make since of what was going on, but after all the stuff he did to me during the process, it just pushed me further away from him. My head was cloudy with years of built-up bondage. I couldn't think straight. It was like trying to take a test with a migraine. Instead of your focus being on everything that you'd been studying to take the test, your focus will be on the pain that you can't get to subside. To answer your question, I say I cheated because I entertained a man other than my husband. That other man became a listening ear and, to this day, is one of my very good friends. Just to be clear, I never had sex with two people at one time. Although that is the picture painted of me, it is not true.

Eventually, my male friend and I scaled back our relationship. We began to focus on why God had connected us the way that he did. My friend has continued to give me business advice and to motivate me to be independent and self-reliant. Although our initial relationship was looked at as wrong, he had helped save my life by allowing me to expand my business. He'll forever remain a special friend. Here's a plot twist. My male friend and I talked about everything. We even talked about how my now boyfriend was a good fit for me and how I should allow him to get to know me. You see, when someone really cares about you, they care about your wellbeing and your growth as an individual. I bet you weren't expecting that. Being open and transparent has taken me to places where lying and cheating could never. That's why I don't do either.

While finding myself, God had given me a dream about a dark brown bottle with a green label on it. From what I saw, it appeared to be beer. In my dream, I drank it, and I liked it. I woke up thinking that this was the dumbest dream that I had ever had. It couldn't possibly have had any meaning to it because I don't like beer. I have never even found one that I had even liked the smell of. If it doesn't smell good, I don't eat or drink it. Later that evening, I had to do an Open Mic session. When I got to the venue, I sat at the bar and looked around at all the beer advertisements on the wall. I thought to myself, "I'm going to order one. They're only $2". After debating back and forth with myself, I decided that I wasn't going to waste my time, money, or energy. I knew for a fact that I didn't like beer so, I didn't order one. I continued my night as usual in the entertainment world, but this particular night was different. There was a gentleman there that I had met early that year. I had given him my business card and told him about Open Mic a few months back. The gentleman would frequent the establishment occasionally and participate in the show. He seemed to be very respectful and not pushy like the other gentlemen who would offer me money and exotic trips in exchange for "my time." So, after my set was complete, he lingered around that night, and we ended up talking while I was breaking down my stuff and preparing to head out for the night. After I was done, we walked outside, and the conversation continued. We ended up talking for a few hours in his car. He was also going through a divorce, so we had a lot in common.

We agreed that we would meet up occasionally and hang out. I didn't have anyone to hang out with, and God knows I could use the opportunity to take my mind off everything that was going on in my personal life. The next day, I called him and asked if he wanted to go to the beach. We had talked about loving the water, so to the beach, we went. That night was the most magical night that I had ever experienced in my life. The next night, which was a Thursday, he invited me to his house to have drinks with him and a couple of his friends. I was apprehensive at first but decided to go. I wasn't a big drinker, and I knew I wasn't going to be comfortable drinking in this man's house, but I wanted the company and needed the laughs. When I got inside the house, a lady and a guy were sitting at the kitchen table. They were drinking some Crown Royal Regal Apple and red wine. I sat down at the table, and they offered me a drink and I said yes to some red wine. As we were all sitting at the table, the gentleman who had invited me to his house opened what I thought was a beer. The bottle was dark brown with a green label. I could smell the sweet aroma across the table. Without any hesitation, I asked him if I could have some of his drink. He poured the drink into my empty win glass. As I put the cup to my mouth, the liquid hit my tongue, and I instantly remembered the taste. I hollered, "This is the beer from my dream". I'm sure everyone at that table thought that I was crazy, but it didn't matter to me. I had received a revelation. I knew that I had connected the dots for what God was trying to show me. The rest was history.

With the sequence of events that had been happening in my life, I knew undoubtedly that my marriage was over. I was working out and eating healthier, and I was finally creating a safe space for myself. I was meeting new friends, and life was looking a lot brighter than it had been in a long time. I had decided that I was ready to move on and seal the deal on the separation but before I did so, I wanted to make sure that my husband was ready to move on too, and that there was no chance of reconciliation. So, one hot and sunny day in July, my husband and I just happened to be home at the same time. I walked up to his truck, and I let him know that I was seeing someone that I was really interested in. I made it very clear that I wanted to take the relationship with my friend to another level. I raised my hand to God; my husband said that he was okay with me seeing another man. I know that sounds completely crazy. It sounds even crazier to me for writing it, but somebody must be honest. This was getting better than a soap opera at this point.

We as a people are lost because we want to cover up our dirt instead of exposing it. I can assure you that whatever it is that you are going through, someone else has gone through a very similar situation or an even worse situation. I choose to be transparent. My desire is to help someone in a similar situation as mine to break free and be healed. Divorce and separation may not be your outcome. Your outcome may not be like mine. God may restore your marriage. I don't wish divorce on my worst enemy. So yes, I encourage all married couples to exhaust all resources before deciding to end their marriage. Most importantly, allow God to tell you to walk away before you leave on your own. One of the most respectable pieces of advice that I got during my separation period was, "Do not involve outside people in your marriage." In other words, don't start seeing anyone until your marriage is over. Unfortunately, life is not as perfect as one would lead you to believe. This is where having a relationship with God kicks in. I wasn't in church every Sunday, and I wasn't living a "Godly life," but God was still speaking to me. He often spoke to me in my dreams. He showed me trying to fix my marriage, and every time, he allowed me to feel the pain and hurt that I would feel if I stayed or how I would feel if I tried to fix it. God was even so detailed with me to show me marriage after coming back after all the turmoil. My dreams were so vivid that I would wake up crying as if I was in the present moment of my dreams. Every time I considered fixing or saving my marriage, God would show me in a dream why I shouldn't go back. God was releasing me. In my time of confusion and uncertainty, God made it plain to me. Go, be free, and don't look back.

I wasn't the only one who had moved on. My husband finally came out of the closet and told me about his girlfriend. He denied seeing her while we were together, but I later found out that that was a lie. Remember the night that I took his phone? Well, the pictures of the text messages that I took were between him and her, and one of the pictures was of her. They had clearly been communicating during our marriage. God confirmed this to me one evening as I was trying to upload an old picture on Instagram. During this time, when you uploaded a picture from your phone to Instagram, it only showed you maybe 8 pictures in your album at a time. That meant that I had to scroll through almost all my pictures. I honestly had forgotten about the pictures until I had to scroll through them, and there it was, plain as day, the picture that I had taken of her name and phone number because it was a female name on his call log. Their text and the picture of her as a teenager. My mouth hit the floor, but my heart healed up a little more because I now knew that I wasn't crazy. I wasn't angry, but God was confirming to me over again that I was where I was supposed to be. I however was hurt. My husband had been going around telling our family and friends that I was cheating on him, and he wasn't as innocent as he had made himself out to be. I decided that I would call him about it, and we had a really long-heated conversation. He told me that they had grown up together in the same neighborhood and that he linked back up with her on Facebook.

Earlier on, I told y'all that Facebook would come back up. My husband wasn't into Facebook, and a mutual friend encouraged him to get on Facebook and share his encouraging messages. I guess he was so encouraging that he snagged him an affair. He said that the woman that he was seeing was his "Customer." So, in my mind, he's using our lawn equipment and our landscaping business to cut the yard of women that he's sexually interested in? He claimed that they were not dating while we were still together, but if you are communicating and spending time with a woman or man outside of your spouse, it is an affair. At the moment, I just wanted him to own it. I wasn't mad at her. I didn't have a reason to be mad at her. What did she do? Nothing. I decided to end my marriage on my own. She was an innocent bystander. My relationship and vows were with him. At this moment, I realized that the reason why my husband decided that he didn't want to fix our marriage when I was trying was because he was emotionally involved with her. I believe this to be true because in the beginning, when my husband thought I was seeing someone else, he specifically said, "I don't care if you are seeing someone else. I want to fix our marriage". At this very moment, his heart was still with me. I don't know and may never know the honest answer about when they made it official, but their conversations started before I moved out of my home in August 2017. I'm completely okay with that.

This brings me back to the point that not everything in life will be done and completed by the "book". I was happy that he had found someone else. In my mind, with a woman in his life, he would have help with our children, and prayerfully, she could cook, and my children would have a real home-cooked meal. Everyone deserves to be happy.

CHAPTER ELEVEN

AFTER THE SEPARATION

LIFE AFTER THE SEPARATION WAS ONE I HAD TO GET USED TO. The difficulty came in when moments happened, and I felt like my husband should have been there. So, here we are, one year later, and our daughter went to the dentist, and the dentist discovered that she needed a couple of fillings. The dentist scheduled her appointment to complete the filling. I took her to the appointment myself. When the dentist started the procedure, he numbed my daughter's gum. He couldn't continue the procedure because she freaked out. He recommended that we see a pediatric dentist to complete the work. So, I scheduled an appointment with the pediatric dentist. I informed my husband about the appointment and how my daughter reacted. I explained that she would need stronger medication to complete the procedure. I had never seen my daughter in so much pain. I honestly didn't know if it was the noise that the drill was making or if it was just her being scared. I'd never experienced having a cavity filled, so in my mind, the only thing that I wanted was her teeth to get fixed and her to be as comfortable as possible during the procedure. I was scared and really wanted my husband there for the next appointment.

A few weeks went by, and my husband and I scheduled an appointment with the second dentist. My husband had all the information for the appointment. We had discussed both of us being there for the appointment and the cost associated with the procedure. During the consult, we knew that the cost associated would have to be paid in advance and that there would be tons of paperwork that needed to be signed.

I showed up to the appointment with my daughter. They gave her the valium and she was all over the place. I thought the medication was going to calm her down, but instead, it made her extremely hyper. She was dancing historically. Falling down, talking crazy, and just would not sit still. At this point, I needed help. Her balance was off, and I tried to hold her. She doesn't want to be held. It's a mess. When she cried and asked for her dad, I didn't know what to do.

I waited and looked at the clock, anticipating his arrival. So eventually I broke down and gave him a call. He explained to me that he was at work and couldn't get off. The whole purpose of us scheduling the appointment together was to make sure that he could be there. My heart dropped to my stomach. Why did I have to call him to find out that he wasn't going to make it to her appointment? All I could think about was, *"How am I going to tell my daughter that her dad wasn't coming to her appointment after he had already told her that she was coming? Why should I have to be the one to break the news to her?"* Life's not seeming fair. Rage came over me. All the hate that I have for this man came back all over again. So, now I sat in the dentist's office, fighting back tears, trying to be strong for my daughter. Needless to say, he didn't show up. The second procedure went horribly. She kept crying, and the dentist couldn't complete the necessary work. She was now to be referred to a dentist who could put her to sleep in Richmond, Virginia, which is roughly an hour or more away from where we lived. This was becoming a tad bit much for me to handle. In the 7 years of being parents together, my husband had never been to any of our children's doctor's appointments. You would think that with him never going to any other kids' doctor's appointments, we would be used to it, but this appointment was different; it was an outpatient surgery. Eventually, reality sets in, and you realize that things aren't the same, and you have to just go with the flow. Whatever that may be.

A couple months passed and we're back at the same place again for the third and final surgery day. The night before, my husband and I had a conversation about our daughter's appointment. We went over the time and amount that is expected to be paid. He asked for the doctor's name and address, and I gave it to him with the expectation that he would meet us there. My daughter and I got there 15 minutes before her check-in time. I can recall pulling up in the parking lot expecting my husband to be already in the parking lot to meet us. I even felt a sense of comfort when I saw a truck that looked like his, only to get closer and realize that it wasn't him. I kept driving, reassured that he would be there shortly. We waited in the car until five minutes to twelve, Still no dad. Surprisingly, she didn't ask for him and I definitely wasn't going to bring any attention to the fact that he wasn't there.

My daughter and I went inside the dentist's office. We sat in the waiting area and her nurse came in to speak to my daughter and myself. She gave us a brief breakdown of the surgery and I sat there thinking we were a little early. Surgery wasn't until 12:30. He still has time to get here. A few moments later, the Surgeon came out to check my daughter's vitals and to have some small talk about her stuffed animal, Elle, and her emoji blanket. With a big smile on her face, she seemed to be doing great and not nervous at all. It was so bad that every male that came through the door resembled my husband. I wanted him to be there. Every part of me wanted him to be there for her.

This time, the doubt had set in, and I knew he wasn't coming. I can say after 8 years of being in a relationship with someone, you begin to learn their patterns. I knew my husband to be a very punctual person and him not being there by this time, I knew he wasn't coming. The surgeon, nurse, my daughter, Elle, and I went to the operating room. The doctor explained to us how the mask with the bubble gum scent would go over her nose and take her to space. First, Elle, her stuffed elephant, had to go to space. Elle went off to space, and my phone started to ring. I looked down at my phone and realized that it was my husband. I quickly apologized to the surgeon and nurses surrounding my daughter, saying it was Dad and answered the phone. I said, "You're late." He then proceeded to tell me that he was at work. He then asked me what was going on. Flabbergasted by his response, I said, "You should be here," and quickly hung up the phone. I was hurt and now holding back tears of hurt and disappointment. I was even embarrassed because everyone in that room heard our conversation. As short as our conversation was, I know my tone of voice told it all. I couldn't believe that he didn't show up. I had heard of so many stories of children dying under anesthesia during dental surgeries. I was already terrified and now that I was having to go through this appointment alone was one of the worst feelings I have ever felt. Now, I was juggling the fear of my daughter not waking up, the pain she was going to feel afterward, and not knowing exactly what to expect.

Most importantly, she didn't ask after him. Having been married for 8 years, there is a sense of comfort in not being alone and knowing that someone is always going to be there. Although we were no longer together, I still expected him to be there for her. This was one of the times I really felt alone & deserted. The fear of having to raise our daughter without her father plagued me, and my heart began to ache. After our daughter was asleep, they escorted me out. I knew I had an hour and thirty minutes to juggle all of these emotions alone. I didn't want to cry in the doctor's office, So I fought back my tears and decided to write my pain out in this book. It didn't mask the emotions, but it helped me to focus on my long-term dream and goal of writing my book and telling the world my story. After a while, you get tired of repeating the same thing over and over, trying to explain to your family and friends what's wrong with you. Rehashing your emotions over and over. This was definitely a different approach for me, but maybe my book would be a resource for someone else.

Later on, that day after my daughter's surgery, her dad called. It took everything in me to pick up the phone. I answered politely. He asked how she was doing, and I proceeded to tell him that he should've been there. He told me that he couldn't get off work and that he was only one person. Now, had that been the case, I would have been more considerate but the fact that he had just taken a nine-day cruise overseas with his new girlfriend just didn't sit well with me. Now mind you my husband never took off work. I had asked him to take off work several times during our marriage. It's been too long to recall all of the dates, but I do remember asking him to take off for our anniversary and even my birthday. It was always a problem. Needless to say, it never happened.

After a pending divorce, everyone seemed suspect. After 8 years everyone and everything is intertwined—family, friends & property. You don't know who's talking to who about what or who had taken who's side. Every failed attempt to vent and get help at the beginning of the breakup was coming up in my mind. So, I didn't want to talk to anyone about how I was feeling. At this point, I was still going to my family church and trying to live life as normal as possible. One Sunday after the church service, a co-labor in the ministry that I was attending, motioned me to come to sit on the back row of the church where we could be alone. She said that she noticed that I didn't look like myself. I was known for my bubbly upbeat personality, and I could see why she would say that. It didn't take much spiritual discernment to see that. This particular Sunday, I was really having a rough day, acting normal and just pretending that everything was okay. I didn't mind because I trusted her. We had spent time outside of the ministry together and served in the ministry together, and I really loved her. Every time I saw her, she was upbeat, and her personality just drew me to her. I enjoyed her company, so quite naturally I trusted her and didn't have a problem venting to her. When I sat down beside her, she hugged me, and she began to minister to me. She made what I was going through relatable to her personal experience and it helped me to open up to her. I began to tell her that my marriage was failing, and I had made the mistake of confiding in a male friend with whom I had begun to have feelings. She prayed for me and told me that she understood and that was the end of that conversation.

Some months later, I was at an all-time emotional high. I had mustered up the strength to host my Annual Benefit Dinner and Comedy Show for my non-profit organization. It was hard especially since I was doing it alone. My husband normally helped me with this event, but this year, it was all on me. I needed to sell 200 tickets to meet my goal. I had no idea how I was going to do this, but eventually, I came up with an amazing or what I thought was an amazing plan to sell these tickets. I came up with a list of 20 people who could sell 10 tickets! This was a no-brainer, right? Well, wrong, it was a flop. I had one person sell all their tickets, one person who made a large contribution. I made just enough money to cover the food and the cost of the two comedians. I didn't have enough money to pay my D.J. or anywhere near thirty thousand dollars to buy the truck that I wanted for the under-resourced individuals and families that I wanted to help. What made it even worse was that the dealership had agreed to allow me to have the truck parked outside the restaurant during my event so that the people who were at the event could see what the truck looked like to gain a visual. I even did an on-air interview with one of my favorite stations, 95.7 R&B.

I just knew that I would meet my goal. Before the show started, one of my family members called me into the bathroom, and she said she had to tell me something. I was curious as to what she was going to tell me. I had no idea, but what they began to tell me blew my mind. The more they talked, the more disbelief I felt. I was told that a mutual friend told one of our family members that I was having a sexual affair with my friend and that was the reason my marriage was ending. She then went on to say that the information was given by somebody from my church. The only person who ran in this particular circle was the minister at the church that I had confided in. I couldn't believe it. Just months ago, I had cried in this minister's arms, seeking guidance on how to fix my life, only to find out that not only did the minister tell my business, but she lied! I never told the minister that I was having a sexual affair. I simply stated that I was having an emotional affair. It was one of the biggest slaps in the face that I had ever felt. Even if I was having a sexual affair, she didn't have the right to tell somebody else. Once again, I found myself feeling betrayed, but this time, it was horrible because someone whom I had confided in was now telling people that I was having a sexual affair outside of marriage.

Unbelievable! I walked out of the bathroom, like the conversation I had just had never happened. I didn't confront the minister, although I wanted to. I felt like it was better to keep it to myself as only one of three things may have come out of that conversation: The minister could have confessed and come clean; two, she could have denied it; or three, we would have been fighting. Either way, I know the truth. I know who I talked to and the source that it came from was my biological cousin and the minister's best friend. Now I know what and whom I'm dealing with, and I'll handle them according. My mother always said, "Some people you have to feed with a long-handled spoon." I soon learned that lesson the hard way. Hopefully, they will buy this book and read it. If you are by chance reading this book, I forgive you for spreading that lie about me. I'll never look at you the same, but I'll give you credit for my success. I am stronger because of you. I don't want anything from you. Not even an apology.

Our life after the separation was so unheard of it was unbelievable. One Saturday, I called my husband and asked him if I could bring my male friend to church. He said that it was cool and he was okay with it. It was important for me to ask my husband if I could bring my male friend to church because although we were mutually okay with seeing other people, we were still legally married. I didn't want my husband to feel uncomfortable in a mutual space. I am always mindful of other people's feelings even when they aren't so mindful of mine. As sinful as that sounds and was, I needed to know what I was working with concerning my male friend and his relationship with God. In my mind, I needed to know how this man worshiped. I trusted the word that would come from the pulpit, and I knew the spirit flowed freely at my church. I had visited my male friend's church, but it was nothing like my church.

Here's a little backstory to pull it all together. Before the Sunday that I brought my male friend to church, I had stopped going to church regularly because I didn't want to see my husband. I couldn't worship in the same place as him. All the memories that we shared, the good, bad, ugly, and indifferent, would flash back through my mind, and instead of focusing on God, I was focusing on my hurt and pain. After the overwhelming number of emotions that came about being in the same place as him, I knew I had to do something drastic. Mentally, I couldn't keep up and people's lives were dependent on me being in a position that I couldn't physically, mentally, or spiritually handle. I decided to step down from the positions that I carried at the church. I knew I wasn't living a Godly life that represented God or my pastors. I didn't want to disgrace them because I loved them so much. I ran away and I hid like Adam and Eve in the Garden of Eden. I needed someone to come looking for me just like God had done them and ask me why I was hiding.

My husband continued to serve in our family church as if nothing was going on. I had introduced him to them. I didn't feel like he deserved to have them, but nobody told me to stop going to church. Moving away didn't help me to spend the time that I desired to spend with my church family. I felt like our separation should have been discussed with the church. If not the entire body at least the leadership team but that never happened. It was like I vanished into thin air, and whatever stories were shared amongst the members became their truths about me and my marriage. I know people were talking because I would often hear about it, and in an altercation with my husband's girlfriend, she accused me of telling people that she was the reason my marriage failed. Afterward, I called my husband, and he confirmed that someone from the church had indeed told her that I said she was the reason for our split. However, that was not true. I never said that she was the reason for our split because she had nothing to do with it. He never told me who said it, but it really doesn't matter because God knows all, and he sees all. I decided to end my marriage, and I didn't end it because I thought my husband was seeing another woman. Maybe we could have reconciled if we hadn't involved other people towards the end of the separation but again, my heart wasn't there. I tried to fix the marriage, but I was being dishonest to myself and unfair to him because my heart just was not there. My reasonings for not wanting the marriage were based solely on our interactions with each other and not growing as a couple or a family. They always say that a woman leaves mentally before she physically leaves, and that was the truth in my case.

After I stopped going to church as much as I had been, I began to see my loved ones forming relationships with my husband's girlfriend. I had nothing negative to say about her until after our altercation which was completely uncalled for. Everyone that I did talk to about her before our altercation can tell you the same thing. I didn't know her and didn't have a reason to not like her. I'm not a negative person and didn't have any enemies before her unless you want to call my husband an enemy. When we had the altercation, it was very alarming to the few that I did talk to about it. I said that to say, I wouldn't expect them to mistreat her because of my relationship with them, but I also didn't expect them to be buddy-buddy with her either. I expected more from my family. When I introduced my male friend to our friends and family at church, a couple of them expressed their mixed emotions and I completely understand that. I didn't want to force him on them and understood that after almost a decade of people seeing me and my husband together, it would be a hard transition. At the service, they hugged my male friend and talked to him with the same love that they would have shown any other visitor. After that point, I didn't see a need to comingle. I realized that I needed to continue growing my new circle of friends with my new male friend. We had our own story to write.

CHAPTER TWELVE
I CAN'T BELIEVE THIS

I WOULDN'T WISH A DIVORCE ON MY WORST ENEMY. It's one of those things that no matter how much you prepare for it, you are never really prepared for it. In my mind, we were both Christians and loved God; there wasn't any reason why we couldn't make this process simple. You know, do it unto God as we did everything else or look at each other as souls that belonged to Christ and split amicably. It didn't happen that painlessly. What I came to realize is that once the decision to split is decided upon, the boxing gloves come off and it's a free-for-all brawl between two people who once proclaimed their love for one another. My intent or goal was never to hurt him or take anything away from him. I just wanted what was rightfully mine. In my mind, I understood that he was my children's father, and I would never want him to suffer because if he suffered, so did my children. I didn't understand how he couldn't see that when it came to me.

When I look back over the tenure of my 8-year marriage, not all days were bad. There were highs and lows as expected but not knowing how to deal with them is what made it bad. Marriage is one of those things that people get hyped up for the glam of it, not realizing that it takes two whole people that become one, not because of the vow itself but because God has created the two of you for each other. The vow is an outward expression and commitment to God and one another. They are merely words that can be spoken by anyone that can speak but the ability to speak them isn't enough to make the marriage successful. When that right one comes along, there shouldn't be any force from the other to be anything other than yourself because you are perfect for each other the way you are. It gels together and mixes into the perfect solution for life—its adversities, trials, and revelations. The mixture is what holds the two together amid the storm. Your consistency is built during the hard times, and the consistency is what determines the foundation that the two of you will stand on. It's what will hold you up, keep your faith, keep you motivated, and be innovative. Marriage takes a lot of work, and you have to be equipped to handle the job. I could tell you about all the great things about marriage but why would I do that knowing that there are not enough people willing to tell the truth about the bad parts of marriage? Maybe if people were more transparent about the beginnings and hardships that they endure during their marriages; we as people wouldn't take marriage so lightly. It takes more than two good people. Two good people won't make a good marriage and I learned that the hard way. We didn't work out together, but that doesn't take away from either of us being good people. We just weren't good for each other.

Divorce brings out the ugly in people. Feeling like the one whom you vowed to be the closest to has hurt you and turned your world upside down brings out the deep-rooted past issues and demons that were suppressed. Whatever is in you will come out. That's why it's important to seek professional counseling and get down to the root of who you are before you even entertain the idea of marriage or before you make any life-altering decisions. Know what makes your heartbeat, understand the rhythm of what makes you happy, and why. We as a people take for granted the things that God has given us freely. When our vision is impaired, we visit the optometrist. Why do we choose not to seek professional care for the most important makeup of our body? Our brain? It's the most vital part of the human body, yet it gets the least amount of care. It tells every organ in our body how to function. I didn't grow up with my parents talking about therapy, and they have probably never seen a therapist or psychologist. Going through my divorce was the first time that I had ever seen a therapist and from that point on, I will see one for the rest of my life. She saved my life.

Walking into my husband's lawyer's office for our judicial settlement conference was rough on me emotionally. It meant that things were getting ready to finalize. We both sat in the waiting room together, and we waited for our lawyers to call us into the conference room. I decided to make light conversation about the cruise that he had taken with his girlfriend. Although it was a very strange conversation to be having with my husband, I was able to put my emotions aside and be happy for him. It was his first cruise, and I was sure that it was an amazing experience for him which he confirmed through our conversation. A few minutes after our friendly conversation, my lawyer arrived, and it was showtime. I went into the conference room with my lawyer and my husband and his lawyer went into another room. His lawyer's assistant offered us donuts and coffee, but my stomach was in knots, and there was no way I could eat anything. I wasn't sure what to expect; I just knew that as friendly as our conversation was in the lobby, it wasn't going to be as friendly in the conference room.

My husband had this idea that everything that we had obtained in the marriage was his. The house, the two vehicles, and anything materialistic. The only thing he wanted me to have was the clothes that I wore. Thank God for the laws the govern a marriage. He didn't want to give me anything, but I knew that "My Vision" had paid off, and I was entitled to half of the equity in the house, the value of the cars, and the landscaping business that I helped start. Without the daunting details, I ended up walking away from two cars, the house, the business that he claimed he wasn't operating, which was a lie, and spousal support. What it boiled down to was choosing to fight over materialistic things or being able to take my children out of state with me. His words were, "If you give me the house, then you can take the kids." That was a no-brainer to me! I choose to give up my rights to "My Vision", our house just to be able to move out of state with our children. We agreed to keep our own debt, and that was that. This meant that I had to start all over with nothing, but most importantly, I had my children. Not even a week later he had moved his girlfriend into our house.

After the Judicial Settlement Conference, it still took almost a year for the divorce to be finalized because he refused to pay the back child support he owed. That following November 2018, we had court and my husband agreed to a settlement amount that allowed him to pay half of the owed amount for back child support. Once he agreed to handle the back child support, our final Divorce Decree was supposed to be drafted by his lawyer and sent to the Judge so that he could sign off on the divorce. That evening, I received a call from my husband.

During this call, he addressed our marriage and apologized for his part in the demise of our marriage. He said that things went too far, and he didn't want this to happen. We both agreed that things went too far. After a moment of silence, he goes on to say that he wanted to tell me and the kids that his girlfriend was pregnant. He didn't want anyone else to tell us; I respected him for that. We had been separated for over a year and both happily dating other people; however, I didn't expect him to procreate during our marriage. I was hoping that he would have done things a little differently than he had done with me. I often said that if I had not gotten pregnant and had taken the time to really get to know him, I would not have married him. Although we weren't together physically, I did care about his well-being because his well-being affected my children. I wasn't complaining either; the idea of him having a stable woman in his life made me feel more comfortable with him keeping the kids as I was the one who provided their daily care. I can remember thinking, "What will he feed the kids when he has them? Ramen Noodles, Hotdogs, and Pizza?" I can laugh about it now because the kids were saved by his girlfriend. She can really throw down in the kitchen. Wait a minute. I guess you're wondering how I know that.

This book wouldn't be complete if I didn't give the full picture of this dysfunctional four-way marriage. My husband thought it was a great idea to throw our daughter a birthday party at his girlfriend's house. I was told by him that it was just a family dinner and that some of his family would be there because it was his turn to host a family dinner for the month. When he brought it up to me, I was a little confused because he mentioned there being gifts for our daughter. I questioned him about it because I wanted to know, "Who brings gifts for a family dinner?" He brushed it off like it was nothing, and the conversation ended. I was out to eat and I got a call from his girlfriend and she's inviting me to her house for dinner. I was told that it was going to be a family dinner and that they were getting cake and ice cream because it was my daughter's birthday. I decided that it would be a great idea if I went to be able to see the women who would be interacting with my children. I would be able to find out where my husband had been keeping my children on his weekend visits without letting me know where they were. This was a big issue for me because I had never been the parent to allow random people to keep my kids. I knew from my husband's work schedule that his girlfriend was keeping my kids and not him. I've always preferred to keep my children close to me. I was thankful for the opportunity to attempt to get to know the girlfriend.

I took the opportunity but when I got to the girlfriend's house, my anxiety about the situation got the best of me. A few of her family members were there, along with my in-laws and our godson. Seeing our godson and his sister at the girlfriend's house almost knocked the wind out of my body because, at this point, I was in disbelief. I walked in and I spoke to everyone and I'm giving it my all not to seem completely caught off guard. I was greeted very warmly and invitingly. Her family was very nice. My husband did the introductions of my boyfriend and me. I could tell that my husband wanted to make sure that my boyfriend and I were comfortable, but in a situation as crazy as this, I don't know exactly how comfortable he really thought things would be. We were invited to fix a plate of food, and I must add the food was delicious. As I began to move around the house, I noticed that there were more and more party decorations, a custom cake, party favors, and a piñata. At this point, my anxiety was through the roof, and I was trying to hold it together. I think that I was doing okay until it was time to sing *Happy Birthday*. I watched as my husband's girlfriend walked over to a cake that she had custom-designed for my daughter, lit the candles, and said, "Let's sing Happy Birthday." I sat there in disbelief barely breathing. My boyfriend was sitting beside me with his arm around my waist.

In the moment I felt a little awkward, with my mother-in-law sitting across from me with another man that's not her son's arm around me. I was stiff as a board. Even though it was no secret that we were dating other people, I at least wanted to be respectful. As the song kept going on and on, all I could do was watch in disbelief. I tried to sing to blend in, but I kept getting choked up. My boyfriend could feel my energy; he began to rub my lower back with his hand to comfort me. Maybe he knew I was about to have a panic attack... Maybe he felt my heart racing through my back. Seconds after the song stopped, I panicked and ran to the bathroom. I immediately burst into tears. Eventually, I got myself together. I washed my face and walked out of the bathroom like nothing was wrong. My sister in-law, whom I am very close, must have been watching me because she was there to my rescue as soon as I walked out of the bathroom. I couldn't believe that this man who had known me for 9 years would think that any of this would be okay. If the divorce had been finalized, then this would have been understandable. My whole issue with the situation is that we were still married, and he shouldn't be throwing a party to celebrate the life of our child with his girlfriend for our daughter and inviting me like a guest in our daughter's life, especially after watching everything that I had to go through for 9 months and the delivery of our daughter. I can tell you that nothing about the ending of this marriage was traditional, but this was a complete slap in my face. I had been talking to the girlfriend and my husband about my daughter's 8th birthday party. I had invited them both. I gave them both an option to participate and even scheduled the party around the girlfriend's work schedule so she could be there. In my mind, since we both had moved on; it would be healthy for the kids to see the four of us getting along. I put myself in this situation way before it was time to try to make peace with everyone else while I was still broken, and it backfired.

When the divorce was finalized, I figured things would be better. That's why the phone call from my husband about the divorce on that Friday was so important to me. We needed closure. At the end of the day, my concern was our children and making sure that they had everything that they needed to be whole despite the blow of their parents getting divorced. The only thing I could say after my husband told me that he was having a baby with his girlfriend was, "Congratulations." I mean, what else was I supposed to say? I was very confused by his announcement, especially since he and I had agreed that neither of us wanted any more kids. After he got off the phone with me, he asked to speak to the kids, so I came back into the house, gave the phone to the kids, and went about my business. A few minutes later, my son ran up the stairs and said, "Mommy, my daddy is having a baby." Our daughter said nothing. I was confused once again. I know that distance doesn't allow for immediate in-person conversations to happen, but I didn't expect him to tell our children he was having a baby over the phone. What was the rush?

The next day was Saturday. My boyfriend and I had taken the kids to the waterfall at a nearby park, and I thought it was so cool that I told the kids to Facetime their dad so that he could see it too. When he picked up the phone, he was so excited to share his good news that the kids didn't get the opportunity to really share with him about what they were seeing. He asked the kids to both get in the camera because he had something that he wanted to tell them both, and he shared with them that the baby he was having with his girlfriend was a girl. My son was very excited; however, my daughter had no response again.

That following Monday, the texts and phone calls started rolling in. My husband and his girlfriend had publicly announced that they were having a baby, and it was a girl! Normally, a woman is between 16 to 20 weeks before a doctor will determine the sex of the baby. She had been pregnant for a while. The rush was they were having a gender reveal that Sunday. Being married for 8 years you accrue a lot of things together like, "Mutual friends." My husband and I had over 200 mutual friends via Facebook alone that we personally knew. I had people sending me messages on social media asking about my marriage because I had never posted anything about a divorce. A lot of people were very confused. I chose not to publicly announce the separation because I didn't think Facebook was the place to do that. I took all my bottled-up emotions and put them in Word to start this book. A slap literally in my face was the Facebook pictures of my husband and his girlfriend's gender reveal that popped up on my Facebook timeline. I would've never seen the pictures, but my childhood friends and family were tagged in them because they were there. I felt like I was being stabbed in my back. These were friends that I'd known most of my life and that I had shared intimate occasions of my life with weddings, baby showers, housewarming, and most importantly, my family. These were the same people who once celebrated me and my husband's baby showers, now attending my husband and his girlfriend's gender reveal, knowing we were still married. There were people from our family church commenting, "Congratulations, I'm so happy for you." Wait what? Again... it was like a boulder being thrown at my chest.

    One of the children that I had before my marriage who my husband had raised for 9 years saw the pictures and told me about it. It was heartbreaking to find out that that was how my child found out that her stepfather was having a child. No one took my feelings or my children's feelings or thoughts into consideration. No one checked to see how we were dealing with the situation mentally. This was just a confirmation to me that some of the closest people to me never took the time to see how I was doing mentally, spiritually, or physically. I no longer needed those relationships as I once did because there was no recovery from that. I was in one of the biggest spiritual battles of my life alone. I guess the assumption was I had a boyfriend, so I had forgotten about the last 9 years of my life and was healed. That was not the case. While I, however, was not in love with my husband, and I no longer wanted to be with him, I was still emotionally scarred by what happened in my marriage, and I needed a lot of support. Everything between my husband and I happened very quickly, even our separation. It seemed as if every opportunity he got, he would just throw salt on an open wound. This woman literally walked in my shoes. I didn't care about her being with my husband, but I cared about her being in our family home, in our family church, and becoming friends with my family and friends. This just seemed too unbelievable. It was like watching a reality show on TV, except my life was taken from me, and I was being replaced with a new cast member. I told y'all that my husband and I were ordained to be a Deacon and Deaconess right. Well, I be damned if they didn't ordain my husband's girlfriend to be a Deaconess too. They may have been married by this point, but the whole picture was just off to me. She probably had my set of church keys too. Okay, I digress.

After the phone call from my husband telling me that our divorce was finalized, I was relieved that we could both move on and our ties to each other were severed, but something just didn't sit right in my spirit. I believed that we were divorced, then I thought about it. My lawyer had never mentioned that it was finalized, so I had to do a little research. I called the Courthouse, and in fact, we were still married! I was livid! I was upset because after my husband and I split, my side of the story was never told. It was almost as if he was able to move on, like "our family never existed." Very few called to see how I was handling the split, and although everyone knew I had moved on with someone else, as did he, that didn't change the fact that we were married and had been married for over 8 years. I still had feelings and emotions that needed to be addressed.

That December, following the phone call from my husband about a divorce that I thought was finalized but was not, my husband decided to mail out postcards to our family and friends that had a picture of our children, his girlfriend, and him that said, "Happy Holidays from the Walkers." That would have been all fine and dandy, but "The Walkers" consisted of me, my husband, and our two children because we were still married. Apparently, his lawyer had drafted the documents for the final Divorce Decree, but they were incorrect, and the judge wouldn't sign them. The judge and his lawyers went back and forth a few times to get the issue resolved. Our divorce wasn't finalized until January 2019. We were married when she got pregnant, married when he proposed to her and married when he sent out family pictures with my children and his girlfriend. Now, let's add the topping on top of the cake. They had marriage counseling while we were married because they got married a couple of days after the final divorce decree was signed by the judge and actually official. Obviously, I was not there but the timeline of events proves my point. I would love to be wrong, not that it even matters at this point in my life.

CHAPTER THIRTEEN

MY CHAPTER CONTINUES

THEY SAY THAT TIME HEALS ALL WOUNDS, BUT I DISAGREE. The only true way to heal a wound is to identify what the wound is and confront it head-on. We as people tend to cover up the things that hurt us or the things that we've done to hurt other people. We don't want to confront the problems, issues, or concerns that we have with other people. We have a tendency to believe that, over time, everything will go away. We hold it in and suppress it. The problem with that is that we don't know what our future may hold; we can't predict what situation we will end up in, and we can't control others inability to be sensitive to what we have gone through. That which we thought we had forgotten about or forgiven is simply stored in a part of our brain and situationally forgotten. Meaning that it always comes back up when we are put in a similar situation, or we're reminded of something that we see and or hear.

Where do you think depression, illnesses, and suicidal thoughts originate from? They come from suppressed concerns, problems, and issues that we haven't dealt with. The thoughts and feelings that arise when depression tries to weigh us down or when suicidal thoughts come are the very things that we have to address and handle. Maybe you were like me, and you tried to express yourself verbally, but you couldn't. It wasn't because you didn't try, but maybe you didn't know how to communicate how you felt in a way that could be comprehended and received by the person who was on the receiving end. Maybe the people you were trying to talk to didn't understand you because of their own preconceived notions. That doesn't mean that you were wrong about how you felt. You are entitled to feel how you feel, and no one can take that away from you. You just have to get to the root of the feeling, and once the issue is addressed properly, you will get the proper healing that you need.

One of the things that I ran into was people who had advice and opinions about my marriage, but they had never been in my situation. They formed opinions based on what they thought they knew about me, my husband and our marriage, with no clue of what was going on. They saw what we wanted them to see and listened to what they heard from outside people and lies. I am a very verbal person, and when my husband and I were going through our issues, there were very few people who understood and were actually there pulling me when I couldn't pull myself. I was dying internally, and that's nothing that I had ever experienced before. My body was physically shutting down on me. My appetite diminished, causing me to lose 30 lbs. rapidly. I was nauseated, and everything that I tried to eat would come out like diarrhea for months. I thank God that I wasn't suicidal, but I can tell you that I wasn't far from it. What kept me fighting even when I didn't know how to was my faith in God and the desire to ensure that my children were taken care of. Yes, the children I had out of wedlock at 14 & 16 years old, the daughter I had with a man that I had only been dating for 30 days, and a baby that I hadn't planned and was depressed about having because I didn't want any more children. So, yes, the very things that the world tells us are out of order are the very things that contributed to saving my life.

There is a book that Christians swear by, and when someone ventures off the page a little, they are often condemned to hell. I am not God, and I don't have a heaven or a hell to put you in, but what I can tell you is God is loving, merciful, compassionate, and forgiving. His grace and mercy have kept me in perfect peace. I made mistakes, and I wasn't perfect, but I was God-fearing. No one is perfect, and we all make mistakes. The biggest mistake of all is not living your life to your fullest potential based on what others think about you. You have one life to live, so live it for you.

I no longer complain about the things that I cannot change. I only build on those things. I tell God what I want and work towards those things, believing that He will make a way for me if it is His will. I use the gifts that God has given me to make me better. I follow my heart and I pray continuously until He answers me. I'm not moved by what man says to me but by what God shows me. I have learned to be honest with myself and do what makes me happy, not to take on more than what I am ready for, be true to my roots, and build on a solid foundation. I can only be who God created me to be. If you look back at your past, you will find clues that God has given you. Use the clues that he has allowed you to recall. Those clues will help you to see your future if you dig deep enough. He didn't create you to walk this life blind. You just must open your eyes and focus on you. Don't be easily distracted by what other people want for you. Your relationship with God is the key to your health, wealth, and success.

My ex-husband and I are now officially divorced; this hasn't necessarily made life easier because now, I am stuck co-parenting with a man that I couldn't even stay married to. Everything about us is different, and there isn't much we harmoniously agree on. I honestly feel like he hates me, and he told the kids that I broke his heart. I am sorry that I broke his heart. At this point, many years have passed, and we've both remarried. I have honestly forgiven him for all the things that we went through in our marriage. My ex-husband's wife remains an innocent bystander in my eyes and their daughter is beautiful. I have a love for her, just like the children that I have given birth to. My desire for our new blended family is that we will be able to co-parent peacefully without any deep-rooted issues from the past. At the conclusion of this book, the children that I share with my ex-husband are currently fourteen and eleven. So much time has gone by and we still haven't found that peaceful place. We constantly go back and forth to court, but I believe that one day, we will get there. Maybe the next book will be on effective co-parenting. Who knows. See you soon!

I would rather spend my entire life making mistakes versus living my entire life in the same place because of fear.
— **Latoria Danielle**

www.ingramcontent.com/pod-product-compliance
Lightning Source LLC
Chambersburg PA
CBHW020337010526
44119CB00001B/16